This book

CHAR

STANDARDS IN THE SERVICES INDUSTRY

STANDARDS IN THE SERVICES INDUSTRY

BRIAN ROTHERY

Gower

Published by
Gower Publishing Limited
Gower House
Croft Road
Aldershot
Hampshire GU11 3HR
England

Gower
Old Post Road
Brookfield
Vermont 05036
USA

Brian Rothery has asserted his right under the Copyright, Designs and Patents Act 1988 to be identified as the author of this work.

British Library Cataloguing in Publication Data

Rothery, Brian
   Standards in the services industry
   1. Service industries – Standards
   I. Title
   338.4'0218

ISBN 0 566 07837 6

Library of Congress Cataloging-in-Publication Data

Rothery, Brian.
   Standards in the services industry / Brian Rothery.
      p.   cm.
   Includes index.
   ISBN 0-566-07837-6
   1. Service industries—Standards.   2. Service industries–
–Management.   I. Title.
   HD9980.5.R687 1997
   338.4'0218—dc20

96–38968
CIP

Typeset in Trump Mediaeval and Helvetica by Bournemouth Colour Press and printed in Great Britain by the University Press, Cambridge.

Contents

Preface   vii

Part I   Services and Standards

1   The context   3
2   The fast track approach   7
3   The full system approach   19
4   The Register of Regulations   27
5   The quality management system   35
6   Honesty, the best policy   43
7   The environmental management system   51
8   Health and Safety   61
9   Who needs standards?   69

CONTENTS

Part II   The Quality Management Documentation

Introduction   77
Sectoral codes of practice for ISO 9000   85
   Hotels   86
   Supermarkets   95
   Manufacturers   99
   Service stations   100
   General dealerships   107
   Retail stores   107
   Solicitors and the legal profession   112
   Accountants   115
   Banks   117
   Restaurants   118
   Other codes of practice   121

Part III   The Environmental Management Documentation

Introduction   125
Sectoral codes of practice for ISO 14000   131
   Print and packaging   131
   Transport   134
   Shipping   137
   Waste management   143
   Retail   144
Postscript: What next?   147
Appendix I   Quality procedures manual   153
Appendix II   Issue identification checklist   169
Index   175

Preface

Precise standards and specifications are now employed by manufacturers world-wide, and they are about to be introduced into services. Not all manufacturers liked them, and many small manufacturers are still falling by the wayside because they cannot fully implement them. These precise standards and specifications will be even less popular in services.

The concept of exact specifications being applied in a standard manner to all components, raw materials, processes and finished products seemed right for manufacturers, and less relevant to services, but now that concept is being extended to services. Buyers of materials, components and finished products demand these specifications from manufacturers, as does legislation in most cases. Large buyers of services, the public, the need to avoid liability, the pressure for conformity, and the use of agreed codes of practice are now beginning to demand them from service providers.

It is much more than the extension of ISO 9000, the quality management standard, beyond manufacturing into services, but the very development and evolution of specific standards, or specifications, for individual services, manifested in such well-known activities as serving or mending or delivering, from takeaway or luxury hotel, service station or hospital, cab or airline. But these standards are about to be manifested also at each of the steps which make up these services, the reception desk, waiting room, meal courses, billing, arrival times, and customer feedback.

Just as the advice about 'staying safe' in this book is directed at teacher, not pupil, so is the whole book directed at trader, service provider, whether greengrocer or hospital general manager, and not at the so-called consumer. The system proposed here is derived from those developed in other books by this author for manufacturers. It is simpler than the systems for manufacturers where quality, environmental probity and safety demand treatment as separate issues. In services the concept of 'quality' much more easily embraces all of these, so that a single system can be provided for the management of the critical elements of quality, environmental probity and health and safety.

While this book is driven in the first instance by the concept of quality in services and the coming ISO services standards, in short satisfying the customer, the services reader deserves a significant amount of advice on how one can use the standards to guard against a less glamorous development than an unsatisfied customer – that of the prosecuting inspector or the opportunistic compensation claimant. Indeed, an accurate, if somewhat vulgar, description of this element commonly used in industry is 'cover your ass'. Here it is also called 'stay safe'.

How the book is structured

For ease of access the book is arranged as three main Parts, followed by a short postscript, which speculates on where standards will spread to next, and two appendices with some detailed documentation and a checklist.

Part I of the text contains discussion or exposition material in nine chapters. Parts II and III are concerned with documentation relating to quality management and environmental management respectively. For many readers the documentation is as important as the exposition, and for some more important, as it above all demonstrates what the standards and regulations require.

This may well be the first book about what is clearly an important new development in standards. I hope that it will help services companies to implement manageable systems of quality, environmental probity and health and safety.

Brian Rothery

PART I

Services and Standards

1

The Context

ISO, the international standards organization, is predicting that services standards will be the 'hottest' area for standards development over the next decade. Services account for 20 per cent of world trade and are experiencing a huge 8 per cent in growth, greater than manufacturing and agriculture. By 1995, cross-border services accounted for 30 per cent of global trade between countries.

During the past ten years, product, process and management standards have enveloped manufacturing industry. At the same time, manufacturing industry became highly regulated, with much of the regulation being enforced under threat of both company and individual manager fines and even imprisonment for breaches of the law and for negligence. This took place alongside the so-called 'quality' revolution, represented by the international quality management standard, ISO 9000, which has perhaps become the world's most famous standard, and the new flagship for ISO, the international standards organization, headquartered in Geneva and with member standards bodies in 100 countries.

The two movements, in parallel rather than complementary, were quality to satisfy the customer, supported, or represented, by ISO 9000, and the need to meet rigid new environmental and health and safety requirements, supported and represented by codes of practice which are now being formalized into ISO 14000, the environmental management standard. While the first, ISO 9000, is mainly customer driven ('if you don't have ISO 9000, you cannot sell to me'), it also has some compulsory legal elements which companies are happy to be able to manage under it, and these are in the areas of product liability, consumer legislation, and general trading and contract law.

A simple view of the relations between a standard and a regulation is that, while the latter is compulsory, it is not practical to meet its requirements without a standard; indeed, within the European Union (EU) the regulations often name the standards. While ISO 9000 and ISO 14000 are overall management system standards, for the system not just the thing, there are hundreds of subordinate product and process standards.

In addition, many regulations and market demands, such as those from large and sophisticated buyers, require independent, third-party, verification that one's products and systems do actually conform to a standard. The act of achieving this verification is called 'certification', a process supplied by agencies separate from, but often close to, the standards bodies.

Now, this process, already under way in services, is being accelerated by a number of drivers – the plans of ISO to develop individual standards, or codes of practice, for specific services sectors, such as healthcare, hospitality, retail, banking, and general services; the spread of ISO 9000 as an overall quality management system into the services sector, and the increasing demand that service suppliers achieve ISO 9000 certification from large industrial buyers (for canteen services and security for example); increasing expectations from buyers at the 'consumer' level; and the development from within service sectors of industry codes of good practice.

At the same time as this 'quality' revolution is under way, the services supplier is increasingly under threat from two forces, the law and the opportunistic compensation claimant. It seems that an honest trader can attract a criminal or civil action more easily than many a common criminal.

Perhaps the most pressing requirement for management, and for individual managers, is to know what is required to stay in business, both by customer and statutory authority, and to know how to implement and maintain a system which will ensure that those requirements will be met rigidly and on a continuing basis.

There appears to be one practical way of doing this, if managers are to maintain service quality and, both corporately and on an individual basis, avoid either real or spurious charges of negligence, and this is to use international management standards, and their related certification schemes, to manage the systems which ensure that all the requirements of the rules are met. The systems controlled under the international management standards in turn ensure the meeting of both the legal requirements and those of customers or industry codes of practice.

US subsidiaries around the world are hearing the following message from corporate headquarters, usually in the form of an impending corporate audit: 'Implement the international standards, implement the local or regional health and safety and environmental regulations, and if there are other local laws or industry codes of practice which apply to your activities implement them also.'

All services companies are operating in an increasingly regulated environment with dangers for both companies and individual managers, the greatest of which appears to be getting caught in a situation where it can be claimed that a company or individual manager has been negligent. As this is being written, there are books appearing in book stores written by solicitors, some self-published, and advertisements in the classified sections of the press, urging employees to watch out for opportunities to sue their employers if loopholes in management systems allow it, and urging members of the public to ascertain if they may have been the 'victims' of an accident with a potential for compensation. Many of the advertisements carry the revealing messages that the legal support will be on a 'no win no fee' basis and that 90 per cent of all such claims are settled out of court. And while real accidents are the given reasons, the opportunity to jump on to financial bandwagons can be read clearly between the lines. Some of these advertisements are an indictment of our modern legal system and reveal the extent of opportunism in the practice of law.

The sophisticated new standards and codes of practice which are now emerging will, if followed to the letter, create a best code of practice situation for any company which will stand up in court as there cannot be better 'expert witness'.

This point is very important, as it applies to any potential threat from within or from outside a company. Legal people and outside activists are not in a position fully to understand either industrial operating environments and how they relate to statutory instruments and good codes of practice. An employee might know this specifically in relation to his or her own area of activity. The reason for this difficulty for outsiders is that all the legal implications of industrial activities are task-, or process- or material-based – in other words, you have to know what is going on at all levels from raw material sourcing through shop floor processing to ultimate product use and disposal. A particular food raw material going into your sausages for example could determine which two out of 104 national food regulations are involved. The lifting of one kind of pallet by a pregnant worker could infringe one regulation but not the lifting of two other kinds. These are called 'issues' in the management systems, and knowing and managing the issues is paramount to safe management.

We can also describe our present trading and services environment as one of heightened accountability. A high state of accountability exists in all spheres of industry, from manufacturing to air traffic control, from the high street marketplace to the scientific laboratory. Without systems of standards and measurement, our modern technical world could not exist, nor could our forms of daily works and commerce. Those parts of our lives involved with work and the commercial marketplace are highly standardized and regulated with visible systems of accountability in place from the weighing scales to the specification on the package. Backing up these standards in the commercial world are stringent legal regulations under such headings as product liability, public safety, consumer protection and misleading advertising, and, increasingly, environmental probity and health and safety. This creates a state of high accountability in our industrial and commercial activities, and has already made dishonest dealings and cheating difficult, if not, in many cases, impossible.

2

The Fast Track Approach

The fast track approach outlined here is a 'services recipe' specially designed by the author for readers who need a quick fix for both their quality and legal protection systems. They might for example want to read and act on this first before considering the other material in the book in more detail. It is *not* recommended as a stand alone system, but as an initial appraisal and method of early action. Only a full system can provide some or all of the protection one needs in today's demanding and litigatious commercial environment. Even the full system described in Chapter 3 assumes that readers will ascertain the required legislation in their own regions, although suggestions are made about how to do this.

A two track approach is recommended for all companies, but particularly for small services companies, struggling to cope with all the demands of the quality, environmental and health and safety standards and regulations – the fast track and full track (more complete system).

The fast track approach to implementing a management system is recommended for all companies, in the first instance, as the management overview and monitoring system for those large services companies who are also implementing the complete, or full track, system, and as a practical fast track approach for smaller companies who may not have the resources, or feel the need, to implement a full system, at least for the time being. What is the difference between the fast track and full track systems?

Fast track is an overview module only. Independent third-party certification of such standards as ISO 9000 and ISO 14000 will not be possible for a fast track module only, so that, in the event of a court action, one will not have the expert evidence and protection offered by such certification. So what use is it then? It is extremely useful if one finds that it is the only way to ensure that one knows what the customer requirements and legal threats are, and ascertains by using the steps necessary to meet these and to protect oneself.

Why would one not adopt the full track system?

In the best of all worlds this author might say that everyone in business should adopt a full track system which will lead to third-party certification that one has adopted ISO 9000 and ISO 14000 standards. In the current regulated and litigatious climate, one is tempted to give such advice, and indeed that climate is worsening.

This author, however, is aware that it would be worse than facetious, if not irresponsible, to tell small service companies to implement standards, let alone have them certified, which would suffocate their systems with bureaucratic documentation and control procedures, not to mention the costs. The fast track approach is an attempt to provide the small services business with a 'manageable' management system. It is simply the adoption of a recipe for services without implementing full management systems to either or both the ISO 9000 and ISO 14000 standards. The 'Grand Slam recipe' is the title the author has given to the fast track system designed for services companies.

The 'Grand Slam recipe'

There are four steps only in this recipe for services companies. They are:

1   know the law
2   write and implement the procedures
3   train the staff
4   implement the controls.

It may help to be clear to the point of repetition about what is being recommended here. No matter how small your operation, and unless you employ trusted family members only, the recipe given here is essential if you are to have at least some of the legal protection offered by the Grand Slam system, irrespective of achieving the necessary quality characteristics and environmental probity. Even with loyal family members only involved, you will be dealing with such third parties as your customers and suppliers and need to know what risks if any are involved with these.

How does one identify the baseline above which one needs a formal system? Is it above street hawker but below family business with more than six persons employed? There is a better indication and it is not related to size or operation, but to the wealth of the person at possible risk. The blunt question is, 'Are you a financial mark?'. Are you worth suing in a civil action? If you have no property or savings, or if your spouse, who is not a business partner, owns it all, you are not a mark and therefore not at risk of being sued in a civil action, or finding yourself the victim of a contrived compensation claim, or, worse, victim of a conspiracy to bring criminal charges against you, at taxpayers' expense, so that subsequent civil action will be made more successful. If you are not a mark, you are unlikely to be conspired against and virtually certain not to be the object of a civil action. One telephone call from your solicitor to the solicitor of the conniving plaintiffs informing them of your financial standing should end any such civil action.

So, from this point, we will assume that you have some standing as a potential financial mark and that you are in a business, however small, involving staff, premises, suppliers and customers, and we will examine what the Grand Slam approach means for you.

1   Know the law

In particular, know those pieces of legislation which relate to your business, not the rest of civil or criminal law which would relate to you as a citizen and which apply to all citizens. It is also convenient to include some virtually mandatory requirements which, while not made compulsory by law, are necessary in the correct performance of one's business, chiefly, in the context of service, the customer expectation of service level, or what is also known as 'the quality of the service' as expressed in a system implemented to an ISO 9000 standard. A non-customer example might deal with insurance levels. We can call these policies as distinct from legal requirements, but so important that they might as well be treated as such.

In the services sector the law as it may relate to your business can be broken down as follows:

1.1   laws relating to products and materials employed
1.2   laws relating to the service and its description
1.3   laws relating to workers
1.4   laws relating to customers or the public
1.5   laws relating to the limitation of your personal liability.

Important note

As one book cannot deal with all the laws in every region in the world as they relate to a service business, this is merely a guide. It is useful as it is material, task or activity orientated, which means that these are the identifiers of the relevant laws, not the statute books, and, remember that your solicitor or lawyer will not necessarily know that specific material you are using or the activities you are engaged in. This also uses EU laws as the model to a large extent with additional tips for US readers. It is important therefore if you are using this as a methodology that you identify your own local or regional laws as they relate to your materials and activities.

1.1   Laws relating to products and materials employed

Assembling this information is virtually automated under an ISO 9000 and ISO 14 000 system in the procedure called vendor management. Vendor here means the supplier or provider of materials, products or services to the services business. Central to vendor management is that each product supplied should be manufactured to a specification, which is fully elaborated on in a document from the vendor. That specification should contain all of the descriptive data relevant to the business, such as weight, dimensions, volume, strength, constituent materials or parts, and so on. It should also contain, where relevant, any information necessary to safe handling, use or consumption, and legal requirements.

When there are environmental considerations, the same or a separate specification should give details of origin, life cycle assessment (that is the 'cradle to grave' description of the environmental probity of each step in the process of producing that product, such as from farm to factory), packaging materials used, and instructions concerning the ultimate disposal of waste related to the product or its packaging.

The particular legal regulations which this approach should ensure adherence to are product liability, laws relating to food and drink, to pharmaceutical or other services with regulated products, including the equipment used in the carrying out of such services, the handling of dangerous substances, if relevant, and certain environmental regulations. And of course normal contract law, here and below.

1.2 Laws relating to the service and its description

A number of services have laws regulating their operation, chief amongst them perhaps being healthcare, transport, hotels, catering, and educational establishments. The usual approach to ascertaining these is to obtain a list from the national or regional professional association or trade body representing one's business. Should that body not have them, this perhaps will be the most significant evidence of the uselessness of that body, and one may need to consult a solicitor.

All services companies need to examine the implications of legislation covering consumer rights and, in particular, in the case of services, misleading advertising. If little else in legislation is of interest to a services company both misleading advertising and everything under the following section should be, as they affect all services companies, large and small where the laws apply.

1.3 Laws relating to workers

These laws could constitute the most important subject in this book for many readers. If one worker only is employed, a services company needs to know what laws could be broken or what real or contrived situations could arise under the health and safety legislation.

Worker health and safety is covered in more detail in Chapter 8. And see below at point 2, 'Write and implement procedures'.

1.4 Laws relating to customers and the public

There is a good rule in manufacturing applicable also to the services sector. Treat all people on your site, whether customer or sub-contractor, or visitor, as an employee. Look, for example, at the way all visitors to certain plants must wear hard hats. If it is dangerous for your staff to do something, it is more dangerous for your customers or visitors. This bit of the task is, of course, made easier by the fact that customers will be banned from the processing areas. They will be in the restaurant, not the kitchen, in the hospital ward, not its generator room, around the boxing ring, not in it.

The big threat for the services operator here is from the customer who, accidentally, or in a contrived manner, suffers an injury, real or imagined. There are a number of safeguards against this and they too can be listed:

1 know the risks
2 write the procedures
3 'broadcast' them to the customer
4 implement controls.

Once again, one should take a sectoral approach and look to one's professional association for a code of practice. If this is lacking, draw up a code using the safe workplace regulation details which specify all of the aspects of a business which could contain risks to workers (see Chapter 8). Write out the 'dos and don'ts' for customers, for staff to implement. Broadcast these to customers through clearly seen signs or other instructions, and implement whatever controls are possible, from alarm bells to supervision.

If some customers do manage to puncture themselves in the eyeballs while smelling your roses, at least demonstrate that the rest of your operation is well managed, but, ideally, do not have roses in the first instance. They should be eliminated at the 'know the risks' stage.

1.5 Laws relating to the limitation of your personal liability

The chief one here in most countries is ensuring that you are operating as a limited company, or one which similarly reduces or eliminates your personal liability, in the event of an action against you. Remember that even if you are highly efficient, an incompetent staff member could cause an action for damages against you. Apart from trading fraudulently or recklessly, limited liability status and the protective measures listed in the other paragraphs above, together with honesty in dealings with customers and suppliers, should give you most if not all the protection you require. If your liability is not limited through the registration of your company, do not operate the business yourself unless you have family staff only and are not a financial mark.

Be careful also if not registered to check the legality of trading under names other than your own, as most countries require trading names also to be registered.

2   Write and implement the procedures

Here in this part of the fast track approach you have an opportunity, should you wish, to go the whole way and implement a complete system.

The difference between the two is largely documentation, although fuller documentation can reveal procedures and controls not obvious in the fast track approach. Here, however, we will concentrate on the minimum amount of written procedures needed to implement an effective fast track system. First, however, the other documents which will be needed from outside the business are considered. (We are not at any stage here dealing with routine accounting, company legal incorporation or annual return procedures, but with quality, environmental, and health and safety matters.)

The documentation (or procedures) brought in from outside can be regarded as the benchmarks or policies or levels of service to which you must operate, not aspire to, not use as targets, but as *minimum* requirements. The only one of these not compulsory under law is whatever level of actual customer service you set yourself. Treating customers as the law, however, is the best method of ensuring quality performance and ensuring practical controls.

The first set of outside documents, or information extracted from them, is that dealing with consumer rights, consumer information and misleading advertising. If your supplier (vendor) has not provided you with adequate assurance that supplies will never infringe product liability legislation, you may need to look again at that supplier, but in general it is your customer you are concerned with in this first set of documents. The advice is not to rush out and purchase copies of the statutory instruments, but to obtain a summary of their requirements either from your trade association or the nearest consumer information office. Chapter 6 spells out what you will need to provide for, or protect yourself against, in a typical country in the developed world.

The next set of documents are somewhat more demanding. These deal with staff health and safety, and in many countries now including Europe, North America, Australia/New Zealand and the Pacific Rim, they carry risk of fines and even imprisonment for individual managers and are full of potential for real or contrived charges of negligence and claims for compensation. These are the actual statutory instruments dealing with worker health and safety legislation. They contain the lists of 'dos and don'ts', often in attached annexes, which can be acquired either directly from the statutory instruments or obtained in easily read lists from local national governmental health and safety agencies, in countries where these exist or operate efficiently.

One of the most unsatisfying tasks of a technical writer is having to tell readers that certain vital information is difficult to obtain. The information on what is required under health and safety regulations to protect both workers and employers is not only difficult to obtain in the first instance but difficult to keep up with, as it is changing and being added to constantly. One of the great failings of trade associations and chambers of commerce is their apparent lack of ability or interest in serving their members by providing this information. One of the frustrations for a writer whose books can take up to a year to be published is that the information in the books also goes out of date. This author is attempting to get around the problem by publishing information in a site on the Internet under the title of 'ISO 14000 and ISO 9000'.

In general in the western world employers need to ensure that they know what is required under these regulations for all the issues described in Chapter 8.

The third set of outside procedures are those dealing with one's specific business, and while there may be a few only for greengrocers, there will be many specific legal requirements for dentists, doctors, and service stations. In some countries barbers have to be registered.

This is a very interesting area as some sectors are so well developed that codes of practice (a subject fundamental to this book) have already been established, either by a controlling authority, such as a professional association, or a sophisticated central franchise owner or licenser or supplier. Two excellent examples of the last are service stations, operating under a single oil company set of standards to a prescribed code of practice, and public houses operating to a code of practice set by a brewery.

The next statement may be the most important in this book. Where there is such an accepted code of practice, that is, how the business should be run, not to implement that code is to invite prosecution and throw away the protection it offers. That code, in particular where it can be verified, through independent certification (from the industry authority or through an ISO 9000/ISO 14 000 scheme) becomes the best code of practice against which it will be difficult to produce a better 'expert witness'. Even where the company has erred, negligence is unlikely to arise.

Another reason for developing this fast track approach is that the author has become aware of the possibility that ISO 9000 may fall into disrepute, from a combination of circumstances ranging from small companies unable to meet it, and over-zealous certification regimes, to sophisticated companies simply giving it up because of either its bureaucracy or its irrelevance. A fast track type system could take over in the services sector initially, as ISO 9000 systems fail to be maintained.

So far we have considered the passive documents saying 'this is the law and this is what you must do to stay within the law'. The next step is to write the procedures to ensure that the law is implemented. Before the reader despairs at this task, he or she can be assured that it may not be difficult. The main task will be to ensure that staff health and safety regulations are implemented and, central to this, and to staying within the law, is to ensure that staff have written procedures and have been trained in them in the first instance. While this may not entirely transfer responsibility for their health and safety from you, it certainly makes them share in this responsibility.

The health and safety requirements can be broken down into three main categories: premises and its equipment, the activities engaged in, and the nature of the staff. The first should be covered to a great extent at the point where the business is first established (if recently) or had its first safety audit and reorganization. It is largely a once-off exercise to lay out the physical attributes – lighting, aisles, exits, and so on. The machinery and equipment must meet the requirements of the legislation for safe equipment and machinery. The main rule here is to insist that the equipment supplier provide evidence that the machinery has been manufactured and installed to the requirements of the regulations and standards. The danger for the business is where equipment or parts of it have been manufactured in house or purchased outside of areas such as the EU or North America. The very act of purchasing equipment outside of the EU by a European company makes that company liable for prosecution should the equipment not comply with such requirements as those laid down under the EU Machinery Directive.

Most service companies can depend on architects and machinery installers to implement those regulations applying to premises and equipment, but should any business use its staff in certain activities normally carried out by specialist sub-contractors, more detailed standard operating procedures (SOPs), such as those used by manufacturers and large service companies need also to be scrutinized. These include activities related to confined spaces, welding, compressed air, steam boilers/pressure vessels, electricity, window cleaning, ladders/trestles/staging, heights and fragile roofs, scaffolding and mobile towers, and exposure to carcinogens. See Chapter 8 for fuller details.

And related to premises and equipment is a stringent legal requirement for safety signs. See point 3, below, 'Train the staff'.

Next, the documentation relating to the activities. All machinery and equipment related activity documentation must either be provided by the machinery and equipment supplier or be based on it if produced in house. It will not be an exaggeration to say that this applies even to the bacon slicer in the corner store. It applies to the instructions in VDU operation, which should have come via the dealer, from the PC manufacturer, and, although it is quite likely that the dealer did not provide them, you as the employer are still liable to charges of negligence and compensation claims for repetitive injury strain (RSI) or eye strain, should your employee believe that either procedures or training were neglected.

Other activities which should be covered by procedures based on the regulations are the lifting of loads, which should apply to many if not all service companies, and the wearing of personal protective equipment, where relevant.

Finally, the regulations dealing with certain persons. The regulations relating to the lifting of loads and hours of work apply to all persons, and in particular to those under and over certain ages, and to persons of certain heights and those with physical disabilities. In all cases where staff have a disability, check all of the health and safety regulations carefully – indeed, consult your solicitor. The handicapped person you went out of your way to employ may be the first to sue you.

The most sensitive regulations applying to persons is that concerning pregnant and breast feeding women. These must be scrutinized and put into practice, particularly in relation to the lifting of loads, rest periods and places of rest and privacy. The great problem with this legislation in certain regions is that while all employers are responsible for applying the legislation, they are not equipped to deal with it where in the first months of a pregnancy the pregnant person decides not to inform them of her pregnancy. This law must be amended to force women at work to declare their pregnancy; otherwise an employer may be in a situation where although 'ignorance of the law is not an excuse' even ignorance of a situation requiring a law is still no defence from contrived claims of injury for compensation.

3   Train the staff

The relationship between knowing the law, writing the procedures and training the staff is possibly best illustrated with safety signs. The legislation dealing with safety signs carries the actual pictures of the signs in its annexes, while health and safety information offices issue booklets with the signs in their appropriate colours. Deciding which signs are needed satisfies one's requirement to know the law, while the purchase and the erection of the signs satisfies those of writing the procedures and training the staff, as the actual signs, being worth the proverbial thousand words, achieve both if properly placed. Only the need for control is left and this can be achieved by regular audits that the signs are in place and a written procedure laying down what disciplinary action should take place if a supervisor observes non-conformances in actions forbidden by the signs or demanded by them. In all other cases when the health and safety or codes of practice, or legislation particular to the industry, apply, actual on-the-job training must take place, in a seminar room or on the shop floor as appropriate.

4   Implement the controls

The last sentences above are an excellent example of why and where controls are needed. A simple schedule of training sessions, for example, can ensure that no new staff member begins certain work until training in that work has taken place, and that all general health and safety training takes place within the first days of commencing employment. The table shows other areas where controls are needed.

Controls needed	Source of information/control
That legislation is up to date	Trade association
Licences for certain activities	The actual licence cross-referenced to a schedule or diary
Staff training	Training schedule
Material or component requirements	Statement of compliance from supplier/manufacturer
Waste removal/recycling	Licence/statement from waste removal company

3

The Full System Approach

As in the fast track approach, the full system is

1   know the law
2   write and implement the procedures
3   train the staff
4   implement the controls.

A good way to appraise your status, to find just how far you have to go in implementing a full system, or whether or not you are legally exposed, is to use the fast track module in the previous chapter for a critical appraisal.

Next try out this checklist for senior managers.

Checklist for senior managers	No	Yes	Unsure
Are you happy that your managers know all the laws as they relate to your activities?			
Are you confident that procedures and controls are in place to ensure that you meet all customer, environmental and health and safety requirements?			
Are you sure that no authority could make a charge of negligence against the company or an individual manager?			
If no, could you be sure that neither will be liable?			
Are you confident that claims for compensation against you will fail?			
Are you in a category where your customer does not and will not demand ISO 9000?			
Are you fully confident that all staff are trained in health and safety matters?			
Is ISO 9000 type quality management of no interest to you?			
Can you ensure environmental probity without ISO 14 000?			

If the answer to any of the above questions is no or unsure, you could use an ISO 9000/ISO 14 000 system, preferably certified. If the answers to several or all are no or unsure you badly need it – indeed, you could be at considerable risk, corporately and personally.

The initial appraisal

Begin with the checklist for senior managers. This will give a general indication of how badly or how urgently you need to implement a full system. For the rest of the initial appraisal use the fast track approach in Chapter 2 as a checklist, together with the issue identification checklist in Appendix II. Remember that these rather general models should be customized to your own business, and in particular if there is an industry code of practice for your business that it be used as a central unit in the checklist to ensure that each step in the code or, better, steps, if you develop higher standards, are audited.

The initial appraisal can be divided into three sections, as follows:

1 the Grand Slam fast track checklist. Use Chapter 2 and Appendix II
2 a fitness for purpose initial appraisal
3 an environmental (including health and safety) initial appraisal.

(The issue identification checklist in Appendix II will also supplement each of the above, so expect some overlap.)

The first point in the list above has already been dealt with. The third is a fundamental first step in the environmental management standard, known as the initial environmental review and so will come as part of the environmental management system (EMS), although the fast track checklist will have already highlighted any glaring shortcomings and may indeed cause such alarm as to assure the implementation of an environmental management system as the first step. We are left now with the need for a fitness for purpose initial appraisal, which could also be known as an ISO 9000 initial appraisal.

Fitness for purpose initial appraisal

There are four broad elements which describe the quality/fitness for purpose of the delivered service. These are:

1 the service description or brief
2 the purchased materials and products which are a part of the service
3 the process of delivering the service (including equipment and facilities)

4 the accuracy or relevance of feedback mechanisms (including customer satisfaction measurements).

The service description or brief

The reasons for the importance of this are spelt out more fully in the next two chapters, but suffice it to say here that for both customer and legal reasons the service brief must be spelt out fully and be exactingly clear and honest.

The purchased materials and products which are a part of the service

The purchased materials and products which are a part of the service are as fundamental as the quality and accuracy of the service itself. Picture bad raw materials being used in the preparation of food being served in an expensive restaurant.

The process of delivering the service

This includes both the things obvious to the customer because they can be seen and tasted, and those less visible from farm to kitchen. It is the manufacturing line supporting the service and the system which brings it to the counter or table.

The accuracy and relevance of the feedback mechanisms

We have only to ask how often in a supermarket we have looked for some mechanism to request that our favourite brand not be off the shelf so often, not to find any such mechanism other perhaps than a young well-meaning but powerless assistant, to understand the importance of mechanisms for feedback, both bad and good, from customers. Such a mechanism is no less than the fundamental 'negative feedback' device which is basic to any healthy organism.

Implementing the full system

There is the question of which part should be implemented first – the quality or environmental, and there is a fuller discussion about this later.

In general the drivers are customer demanding ISO 9000, and legislation and danger of being sued demanding ISO 14000. One large customer using your service might mean your implementing an ISO 9000 system straightaway, while a dangerous or litigatious environment might demand an early ISO 14000 system.

Some will find themselves serving both quality and environmentally conscious buyers, such as large high street retailers who want a green image, and will need to implement systems to both standards.

Apart from the general market and legal considerations, the fast track appraisal may also have revealed which part or parts need to be implemented urgently.

Four basic questions may help in this decision.

1 Is an important customer threatening to de-list you as a services supplier unless you implement an ISO 9000 system? This is still unlikely in the services sectors, particularly if there are many customers or you are selling to the public, but depending on the future growth of ISO 9000 this could change. Also your competitors may offer your customers their ISO 9000 system as evidence of superior quality service

2 Has the appraisal of the health and safety situation revealed inadequacies? If so, this should be the number one priority or at least acted on in parallel with other priorities

3 Are any environmental related activities infringing local authority regulations or national laws, or causing nuisance or pollution to the community?

4 Is there a threat to the community from any potential accident? This is unlikely in most services outside certain utilities such as power supply and transport. If there is, however, this also must receive top priority.

The main steps in implementing the system

The main steps are:

1   implement a quality management system (QMS) (see Chapter 5)
2   build a Register of Regulations (see Chapter 4)
3   implement an environmental management system (EMS) (see Chapter 7)
4   as part of the EMS construct a health and safety system (see Chapter 8)
5   write or acquire and implement a set of standard operating procedures (SOPs) (see Chapter 8)
6   as part of all or any of the above, adapt the premises, layout, or equipment as required by the new QMS and EMS.

Each of these is dealt with more fully in the chapters which follow.

The codes of practice

It may be a considerable help to the reader if the meaning, and place in the system, of the codes of practice are understood. Two figures, one on page 78 and the other on page 126, may help to put it more clearly, and it may avoid much confusion, and be seen to be quite simple if one spends a little time looking at the figures and relating them to one's own business.

Much of the quality, environmental, and health and safety systems are generic, that is the same for all companies. How you plan your system, the documents and controls used, the common issues, the specific regulations applying to workers, are common to all companies, both services and manufacturing. There will be some manufacturing activities, often of a dangerous nature not found in services, but most of the health and safety issues are shared by all.

If the systems are not to be solely sets of bureaucratic procedures, particularly in the case of customer or quality delivery, they have to be also made real for each industry and reflect the actual tasks found on the ground, in the hotel lobby, in the restaurant, in the bank, and so on. This is where we insert the codes of practice into the procedures manuals.

These are the codes which ISO hopes now to formalize into services standards, and these are the codes already emerging within services sectors. In this book some existing codes are used and some have been created or anticipated by the author. The sectors covered are hotels, service or 'gas' stations, dealerships, supermarkets, solicitors, accountants, restaurants, shipping companies, retail stores, print and packaging, transport and waste management, most from the quality point of view, some also from the environmental. Other codes of practice not yet investigated by the author are also mentioned.

The codes of practice can provide the sets of evaluation criteria which should in turn be the basis of the standards, and this is particularly important when the service provider is also the expert in the professional sense. Or as we will see in the Postscript on page 147 masquerades as such. We will also see that many of the sections of the codes are themselves generic – that is, capable of horizontal application across all services, such as complaint procedures, and this book attempts not to repeat these.

4

The Register of Regulations

Perhaps one of the most unfair, and even unjust, legal maxims for people in business is that 'ignorance of the law is no excuse'.

The reason for the injustice is that it has become extremely difficult to know all the laws which may relate to even the most basic of businesses. The ordinary greengrocer now faces legislation for almost all of the products on display, and even how the products are displayed, which includes stringent rules covering display stands outside of stores. In some EU countries standards trading officers prowl the streets, looking for victims upon which to pounce.

This book was written largely in a farmhouse, just purchased by this author and his wife, near the Atlantic Ocean in County Wexford in Ireland. Part of the work on the site was the restoration of a beautiful stone farmhouse barn and its conversion into a study. Just before the completion of the book, a newsletter arrived via the Irish Health and

Safety Executive with information on the continuously evolving EU health and safety regulations. This newsletter reminded readers that teleworkers, and the self-employed, such as this author, were also subject to the health and safety regulations. What this appears to be stating is that if this author refuses to sit in the barn in front of the VDU in the prescribed way and under the prescribed conditions, he is infringing EU and local regulations. This is patently ridiculous as is an increasing amount of EU worker legislation.

This is the kind of over-regulation, supported by over bureaucratic standards, and repressive certification inspections, which is going to fuel a backlash against both standards and regulation. Meanwhile, however, the honest trader has to know the law, or at least that part of it where he or she is vulnerable.

There is a revolution under way in industry and in services, which the legal profession is not yet fully aware of. It is that all industrial activity, both manufacturing and services, is increasingly *compliance driven*. This can be illustrated in a simple manner by comparing the 'drivers' behind the quality management standard and those behind the new environmental management standard.

The quality management standard, in the form of ISO 9000, which is sweeping the world, is voluntary in the sense that it is market or customer driven, not demanded by law. In reality, for those companies supplying large manufacturers, it is actually mandatory as they will be out of business without it. The new environmental management standard, however, is largely compliance driven, as it embraces a number of elements which are required under statutory instruments.

The strength of the new conformance driven interest in environmental management standards is underpinned by the issues which they manage. These are compulsory environmental issues, such as emissions, discharges, noise and odour, staff health and safety regulations, process and public safety, and product safety. Under the 'voluntary' ISO 9000 quality management standard, three other conformance driven issues can be managed, and these are product liability, consumer information, and misleading advertising.

Why not ask one's solicitor to supply a list of the laws one needs to be aware of? Alas, the solicitor does not know and cannot know what all of these are.

The problem for the legal profession in trying to service its commercial clients can be summed up in a single statement: *the relevant legislation is issue and task based*. Whether the question is which of the over one hundred pieces of food legislation relate to the activities of a food manufacturer or what laws were broken in a shop floor accident, the answers are as much dependent on the process, component, raw material employed, and task being undertaken, as they are on one's knowledge of the statutory instruments.

Health and safety, now highly regulated, with severe penalties for infringement, apply to worker, customer and members of the public, and as we have seen above the self-employed. These regulations are issue and task orientated, such as in procedures for handling harmful substances, the kinds of loads staff may lift, safety signs, work equipment, the workplace, and what pregnant workers should not do.

When something goes wrong, which may be manifested in an accident or a major non-compliance with procedures, only a scrutiny of the process or task involved can reveal the extent of the adherence to a code of practice and the relevancy of one or more statutory instruments which may apply to the situation. Examples can be found in such situations as work in confined spaces, hot work, manual handling, personal protective equipment, in each case of which several statutory instruments could be relevant. For both plaintiff and defendant, knowledge of both the general work situation and the specific task are of paramount importance, as these lead in turn to statutory instrument, documented procedure and standard employed.

Both manufacturers and service companies are finding that they cannot get support from the legal profession in the construction of the most basic document needed to ensure that one is in a safe trading situation – the Register of Regulations, which can be a ring binder containing the regulations applying to one's business, the register from which the procedures and controls are established. The legal people cannot know all the raw materials and shop floor issues involved. Does a food retailer, for example, impose requirements on suppliers back to the farm? Was the incident pulley related, fork lift truck related, was it covered by general requirements of the general requirement of a piece of legislation covering factories or by a specific health and safety regulation, or did it involve a listed substance?

More importantly perhaps, were the appropriate procedures written, and the training and controls in place, and were these certified by 'accredited' third parties, where either or both certification and accreditation are relevant?

The few consultants already trying to service sophisticated manufac-turers and services companies in their implementation of environmental management and health and safety systems, are getting new business from simply analysing the statutory instruments, producing checklists and delivering written procedures, audits and control documents.

The first step in protecting oneself is 'know the law'. This can be achieved by constructing a Register of Regulations in a simple ring binder with the actual statutory instruments as they apply to your business inside. The statutory instruments are the acts of parliament or 'laws' or 'regulations' purchased from your local equivalent of Her Majesty's Stationery Office (HMSO) or Government Publications Office. Not all of these are needed, as some can be left to your solicitor, so we shall deal with these first.

What you can leave to your solicitor

Assuming that you are a normal, honest human being, all your normal trading activities will be within the law, so that only a genuine mistake or someone trying to cheat you will involve you in litigation under common or contract law. Should you get into trouble here, your solicitor can handle it without your needing to read or scrutinize statutory instruments.

There are, however, three elements required under law which an ISO 9000 quality management system caters for. These are product liability, consumer rights and misleading advertising. Let us call these customer-related laws.

Managing the customer-related laws

A full ISO 9000 quality management system will manage these in an adequate manner, but here is a simple recipe for ensuring that one stays within the law, in the above 'quality' areas, and avoids prosecution in doing business with customers.

1   Fully specify your service. If you are selling raw materials, components or products, supplied by manufacturers, demand full printed or typed specifications, and maintain them in ring binders. Supply them or show them when asked by your customer. Ensure

that your suppliers guarantee the maintenance of these specifications, and consult your solicitor if necessary on the obtaining of warranties, or consult your suppliers.

Where you are supplying some or most of a service, write an honest and accurate specification. The model or benchmark may be the menu outside your restaurant. Make sure that what is on display is available at the prices shown. Use this specification of your finished service, supported by supplier specifications, as the basis of your quality management system. You are, in fact, now implementing an ISO 9000 system.

2   Never make claims you cannot support, exaggerated claims or false ones – 'open 24 hours', 'no job too big or too small', 'qualified mechanic always on duty', and so on.

3   Use only products and components with correct labels, guaranteed to meet consumer legislation. Check that any required marks are in place – the CE Mark, for example for certain categories in the EU.

4   If your products or components are in categories covered by legislation, ask your supplier for evidence that the legislation is met. In most cases, all the proof you need is that the component carries the mark or standard associated with the legislation. Product areas where this is critical are:

● electrical
● machinery (safety)
● construction
● telecoms
● medical
● personal protective equipment
● toys.

The CE Mark must be shown on the above products in the EU and demonstrates that they meet all of the requirements of relevant EU directives.

If the reader is in a service dealing with a specialized and highly regulated industry such as nuclear, aerospace, medical or airline, industry sources should be consulted for regulations in the first instance and not just this book.

While this book cannot list the service and product liability regulations for every country which it may be read in, the EU serves as a good model, so some further notes on EU legislation in this area are given in Chapter 6.

Managing the environmental and safety-related laws

The Register of Regulations will list all of the required environmental, public safety and staff health and safety laws.

While some specialized services companies, such as those transporting or treating toxic waste, will have specific legislation applying to them, most will face environmental regulations only in the following areas:

- planning
- emissions, including odours
- noise and other nuisances
- waste water discharges
- general waste management.

Each company must either read the relevant local legislation or obtain advice from local authorities, industry associations or consultants and establish the exact requirements, write the procedures, and implement the controls.

The safety-related laws are normally issued by governments in printed statutory instruments similar to the environmental regulations, and referred to as 'health and safety regulations'. There is often a separate national health and safety authority, which issues free information.

The regulations are not always obvious

Unless the operator carries out a complete review of operations, looking at all tasks and at every component handled, all of the relevant legislation may not be identified. A good example here is a service station, or gas station. On top of the necessary quality or customer requirements, there are some obvious public safety issues, covered by law, chief amongst them the unloading or transfer of petroleum from tanker to storage tanks, the procedures for which, although environmental, can be conveniently managed under an ISO 9000 system. While these are obvious, less obvious may be regulations that the service station manager may not even be aware of – for example, if the forecourt store has begun to sell certain categories of food, such as smoked salmon, or exposed fruit or meat, strict hygiene laws may have to be enforced, laws which could have stiff penalties attached to them. A full audit is required.

The legislation should set the lower limits

The legislation should set the lower limits: our policies may be that we meet even higher levels of performance or eliminate all pollutants or waste or undesirable practices or substances in the legislated categories. For example, with an issue such as a certain amount of effluent below a statutory limit or a limit licensed by the local authority, we need to set our own policy limits on the issue and state them here as if they were a regulation (our own). Similarly, if there is an industry code of practice for an issue, a level of service say, we should set this also as our policy, under self imposed regulation.

The Register of Regulations is a passive device, simply attesting to the fact that we know the regulations, so do not try to turn it into a control document. Many of the statutory instruments, however, contain in annexes the actual procedures for operating within the law, although these may also be more easily understood in related standards or codes of practice.

To know the law and to implement the procedures for ensuring that you stay within it, you can get the actual statutory instruments, and by reading the list of 'dos and don'ts' in the annexes at the back of the document you can write your procedures and devise your controls.

Alternatively, once you know the law you can seek simple lists of procedures for you and your staff in the following cases:

- health and safety from your local health and safety authority or from a safety consultant
- environmental from an environmental consultant, but this should be necessary only for service businesses with real or significant issues of emissions, discharges, noise, odour, waste or transport
- process or public safety. If there are such issues, you must be in a

specialized category where there is an expert industry association, which should have codes of practice which you and your staff can adopt as procedures.

A list of areas of sample legislation, codes of practice and policies for a services company in a typical EU member state follows (note that this cannot be comprehensive for all services companies):

- physical planning
- the EU EMAS regulation (big companies only)
- environmental impact assessment (big companies only)
- waste
- toxic waste
- transport
- packaging
- nuisance and noise
- handling of dangerous substances
- shipping of dangerous substances/wastes
- trees, amenities, landscape, and wildlife
- effluent discharges
- emissions
- use of materials
- use of energy
- product quality
- public safety
- health and safety
- raw materials (that is the legislation relating to them)
- supplier/including services activities, such as transport (that is the legislation relating to them)
- product/service liability
- consumer information/rights
- misleading advertising.

(Note that some are codes of practice, and some policies.)

In this chapter we have tried to examine the extent of the legislation applying to services companies. In separate chapters we examine more closely the customer, environmental and health and safety management systems required to ensure that we stay within the law and meet our set policy levels in all three of these critical areas.

5

The Quality Management System

Fundamental to understanding the 'concept' of quality in services, is to replace the notion of 'high quality' with fitness for purpose. An example frequently used by this author is that of glass. One buyer specifies glass which if rushed at by a 200 pound man wearing safety clothes and helmet will neither crack nor shatter. This product is needed for the windows of an office block. A second buyer wants glass which will shatter into harmless round pellets should a nine-year-old girl or boy fall through it. This is for stunt work on a movie set. The quality of the second is no less than that of the first, as both satisfy the requirements or specifications, or are fit for purpose.

Once this incorrect connotation of 'high class' is removed from that much abused word, 'quality', we can get on with understanding what quality standards in services mean. The service can be providing clowns at parties for children, giving body-building courses, operating cheap roadside diners, or tattoo establishments.

Now let us consider at least three different levels of standards in the service. At the lowest level we have the standards of the purchased raw materials and components, in the sense of vegetables or meat for raw materials, and more complete things such as the equipment used for components, which we may call equipment, to distinguish it from raw materials.

At the next level we have the standards for the processes or products of the completed or delivered service – the meal, the delivered parcel, and so on. Finally, at the top we have the quality management system, such as ISO 9000 (and to be precise, one of the standards in the ISO 9000 series).

The top level standard, ISO 9000, is fully developed for manufacturers and being used by them world-wide, and, although still somewhat vague for services, it is spreading also in the services industry. At the lower level, most of the standards exist for the raw materials and equipment, as these have already been established in manufacturing and agriculture – the peas, steak, tables, gym equipment, hotel beds. Now under way for the middle level is the development of the codes of practice and standards for how the service provider goes about completing or delivering the service – how you are treated in the hotel, how your meal tasted and how and when it was delivered, how you were served in the bank, the correctness of your bill, the waiting times, the attitude of the receptionist, and so on. This is where the real revolution in services standards is taking place.

Hundreds of thousands of manufacturing companies world-wide have already achieved the ISO 9000, quality management system, standard, and forecasters are talking about a possible two million companies within the next three years. As already noted, the standard is also beginning to spread rapidly to service companies.

British Standards Institution (BSI) invented ISO 9000 by producing an earlier model with the title of BS 5750. The main purpose was to provide a single agreed standard which would eliminate or reduce what were called 'vendor assessments', which are the carrying out of audits by big buyers on all of their individual suppliers, called 'vendors'. While ISO is international, Europe provided the catalyst for its extraordinary spread in cascade fashion world-wide, when the European Commission instructed CEN, the European Committee for Standardization, to adopt ISO 9000 as the harmonized quality management standard for the single market, which became a reality when the Maastricht Treaty created the European Union.

Where the European Commission was the catalyst, the almost biological mechanism for the growth of the standard was the buyer-supplier interface and the related mechanism of certification. Sophisticated buyers demanding proof of implementation of ISO 9000 through certification schemes ensured both the cascade effect and the horizontal growth. In the latter case, US companies in Europe were amongst the first to adopt the standard, thus ensuring its spread multinationally and back in the US.

While most services companies do not have large buyers with so much power that they can demand proof of ISO 9000, many thousands of service providers do sell to large and sophisticated buyers and they are now experiencing the demand for ISO 9000 certification.

The IBMs of the world, however, selling to the person in the street and to the small dealer did not wait to be asked for ISO 9000 as both their manufacturing and services standards, but went ahead and implemented them, simply because they had a 'best practice' policy, starting a cascade effect where smaller service providers followed their example. Now that hotels and other prestige service suppliers have begun to implement ISO 9000 there is a real possibility that the services industry could begin to divide into the two tiers of ISO 9000 (and its connotation of quality) and non-ISO 9000.

ISO 9000, the quality management standard, is a step beyond the mere acceptance of standard or harmonized protocols: it is no less than a universally accepted method of assessing the honesty, quality, accuracy and competence of one's business to meet certain laid-down specifications for its operation. It is the first sign that one can operate commercially within universally accepted conditions and to a set of agreed standards. It has led to a process beyond advertising and public relations or images of quality, which is third-party verification through the act of certification, and which can involve audits from the inspectors of an accredited certification agency.

Perhaps the most extraordinary thing about it in services is that it has gone a long way towards exposing as a myth our idea that most if not all of our perception of the quality of a service is qualitative, that is, subject only to our own good taste and judgement. It has done this by actually breaking down the steps in both the process of producing and delivering a service, so that we can literally put numbers on them or manage them against checklists. A shocking idea in one sense. Indeed, it would be interesting to sit down and write out a list of what services should never out of decency be measured in such a manner. Religion, art, music, literature? This author would not like to see these subjected to specification. But how interesting it would be to see psychiatrists and therapists made accountable! The witch doctor in the jungle would surely claim qualitative immunity.

There are of course great dangers of bureaucracy. Implementing the standard on a voluntary basis is one thing, but having to demonstrate that one has been certified another. There is more about the act of certification later. The worry is that a demand for certification is being applied by some over-zealous buyers to all suppliers by the imposition of a blanket requirement for ISO 9000 certification on to all of those on their approved vendor listing. This has already caused the requirement for certification to spread to such suppliers as installers of industrial security equipment, who might have no more than six staff, and it is feared that it could spread to others. It is not difficult to imagine state or public procurement buyers imposing blanket bureaucratic buying demands which could include all small service providers.

As plenty of books, including some by this author, deal with the details of implementing ISO 9000, an overview only of the standard is given here. The ISO 9000 series of standards runs to around 20 different standards, the main ones being ISO 9000 and ISO 9004 which in the first instance are used for internal reasons – that is, not necessarily for third-party corroboration, or demonstration of compliance to customers. The two standards also help to explain the series and the philosophy behind them. The services standard has the somewhat awkward title of 'ISO 9004 Part 2'. For practical purposes it is simply called the 'ISO 9000 services standard'. Standards ISO 9001 and ISO 9002 are used when one is seeking external verification or certification. The ISO's own explanation of ISO 9004 Part 2, taken from the standard, is looked at at the end of this chapter.

The essence of ISO 9000 is specification

From a management point of view, ISO 9000 means no more than identifying those key steps which ensure that final production of product or service meets the specification for that product or service. Its essence is specification, whether that be for purchased component, process or finished product, and the key steps which could affect the quality of the finished product or service are rigidly defined and controlled. We have already seen that quality in the ISO 9000 sense means fitness for purpose, but this appears to need constant repetition. Cheap Christmas crackers can be made to the specified requirements, as can frivolous party accoutrements, and both qualify for ISO 9000.

In addition to books on the subject, there are packages of generic documentation available from publishers such as Gower, and, as one would expect, there are a plethora of consultants available to support the implementation of ISO 9000. The first steps necessary in the implementation of the standard are to make the commitment and appoint a quality manager. That manager will have little trouble in taking the next steps, which are to acquire copies of the relevant standards – ISO 9000, or ISO 9004 and either ISO 9001, ISO 9002, or ISO 9004 Part 2, depending on whether one is designing and manufacturing, manufacturing to a given design, or in services. If one is developing software, the standard is ISO 9000–3.

Implementing a practical and good ISO 9000 system requires both adherence to the generic requirements of the standard and to the specific needs of one's process. This is where the codes of practice for specific services come into play, the codes for which ISO now intends to develop specific services standards. Many of these already exist or are evolving. Here are some examples of service industries with codes of good practice:

- hotels and catering
- supermarkets
- transport, storage and distribution
- shipping
- banking and finance
- education and training
- solicitors
- accountants
- service stations (gas stations)
- car dealers
- security installers
- waste managers
- health care.

The best are those published by the British Standards Institution (BSI), but others are published by industry and trade associations, so a way to identify those for your particular service area is to call your industry or trade association. If it does not know about such codes of practice, at least you will know how adequate they are in your representation.

What the ISO 9000 standard has to say about services

The ISO standard which deals specifically with services, or more precisely tells us how to use other standards in the ISO 9000 series for services, is entitled 'Quality management and quality system elements Part 2: Guidelines for services'. Only what is deemed relevant for our purposes in the standard is discussed here.

While one can have sympathy for the authors and ultimate architects of the services standard in their attempts to formalize and quantify elements which have for millennia been qualitative rather than quantitative, an honest appraisal of this standard must admit to its being confused and obtuse. This author has become increasingly convinced that much of the trouble involved in interpreting ISO standards to make them work in the real world is because of the obsession of some technical committees to stay away from specific industry codes of practice, so that pure or generic standards can be achieved. The useless thing we now all call the 'Quality Manual' is a supreme example of this, as is checklist certification inspections of documentation, hardly worth the paper they are written on.

Central to ISO 9004 Part 2 is the momentous statement seen also in the other ISO 9000 standards that 'The service organization should develop, establish, document, implement and maintain a quality system as a means by which stated policies and objectives for service quality may be accomplished.'

This is classic ISO language but staying firmly away from any responsibility of relating this to the greengrocer or hairdresser who may be shut down some day because local authorities may insist that they demonstrate certified ISO 9000 systems.

The operational elements are seen as those which give 'adequate control and assurance over all operational processes affecting service quality'.

Another legalistic statement is that 'The system should emphasize preventive actions that avoid the occurrence of problems while not sacrificing the ability to respond to and correct failures, should they occur.' Here as so often ISO wants it every way.

The list of quality system operational elements is more helpful. These are seen as: marketing, including market research and analysis, supplier controls, service brief (which in the opinion of this author should be of paramount importance), and management of the process.

The standard lists service areas where it expects the standard to be applied and it is interesting to note that, while we are talking about the overall quality management system here, detailed codes of practice are also expected to emerge from ISO committees, and are already emerging within the service industry sectors. The sectors listed in the ISO 9004 standard are:

- hospitality, including catering, hotels, and tourism
- entertainment, including radio, television, and leisure
- communications
- airports and airlines, road, rail and sea transport
- telecommunications, postal, and related
- health services, including medical staff/doctors, hospital, ambulances, medical laboratories, dentists, and opticians
- maintenance, including electrical, mechanical, vehicles, heating systems, air conditioning, buildings, computers
- utilities, including cleansing, waste management, water supply, grounds maintenance, electricity, gas and energy supply, fire, police, public services
- general trading, such as wholesale, retail, distribution, marketing and packaging
- financial, including banking, insurance, pensions, property and accounting
- the professions of architecture, surveying, legal, law enforcement, security, engineering, project management, quality management, consultancy, training and education
- administration including personnel, computing, and office services
- technical including consultancy, photography, and test laboratories
- purchasing
- research and development, and related.

A quality management system (or ISO 9000 checklist)

As the actual ISO 9000 standard documents are quite legalistic, this is an overview of what their various paragraphs demand from a services company.

- a documentation system and its control, including revision and circulation control

- written policy commitment from top management in what is called the 'policy statement'
- an organization, resources, and assigned responsibilities
- a written, fully specified service or quality brief – that is, what is being promised for delivery
- a quality management system, covering
    - the above
    - contract review
    - design if relevant
    - purchasing
    - product or component supplied by the customer or others
    - identification and traceability of the components in the service
    - management and control of the service process
    - inspection and testing procedures
    - control of the inspection, measuring and test equipment
    - knowledge of the inspection and test status
    - control of non-conforming steps in the service
    - corrective action
    - handling, storage, packaging, and delivery
- records of the state and progress of the system
- internal checks or audits on the quality as stated in the brief or contract
- staff training
- statistical controls if necessary.

6

Honesty, the Best Policy

In addition to accuracy, truth is now legislated for in business, in laws dealing with product liability, product safety, service and product descriptions, consumer protection and misleading advertising. As with products, a service should be fit for its purpose, and be properly described whether in advertisement, menu, brochure or catalogue. Even the very language used to describe a service could lead to prosecution if it gives a wrong impression. Amongst the most demanding legislation facing retailers and other services providers, and some of their suppliers, is that covered by various national and regional product liability laws, where liability can be incurred by the producer for damages wholly or partly caused by a defect in a product sold or delivered, irrespective of whether the manufacturer was negligent. The damages can be in the form of personal injury or to property.

Staying with services which deal with the sale of products, for the moment, in the EU for example those potentially liable are manufacturers, their suppliers, including suppliers of both components and raw materials, and certain other persons who may put their own brand on a product. Of particular interest to non-EU manufacturers is that it also includes an importer of products from outside the EU, for example Japanese or US products. The supplier, or retailer, cannot hide behind unnamed manufacturers and will be made liable in the event of not identifying the source.

The most likely reason for a product liability charge to be possible is a breach of safety. All products which are inherently dangerous should deal with safety in labelling, advertising and, where necessary, through the issuance of instructions and user manuals. A very good example is the 1995 Machinery Directive, which is dealt with later in this chapter.

Grounds for exoneration from liability include those defects that arise after the product went into circulation, or where, because of the current state of technology, the defect could not have been known about at the time, or where the overall design of the product causes defects in the component or raw material in question. The producer is not liable if he did not put the product into circulation, even though he made it. Products exchanged as private transactions also appear to be exempt – that is, not made for commercial purposes.

The cardinal rule for avoiding liability on all fronts is to know the law, transform the relevant bits of the law into training or procedural manuals for staff or users, and control this process.

To avoid product liability a services company should handle only those products whose manufacturers give warranties of their safety, reliability and fitness for purpose, and who guarantee that all legal requirements have been met, such as those of the Machinery Directive, discussed at the end of the chapter and those of the CE Mark discussed presently.

Hard on the heels of the product liability legislation come those for consumer information and consumer rights. For example, the EU Misleading Advertising Regulations forbid false or misleading information about goods and services, including their prices, and extend to advertisements, claims by manufacturers and distributors, catalogues, pictures on packages, and even the oral claims of salespersons. It brings criminal law to bear on the maker of the claims, imposing obligations of honesty and truth.

Both manufacturers and retailers can be liable as the legislation applies to the description of products, and the offences are either to apply a false description to goods, or to sell or possess for sale goods to which a false description has been applied. The false description can relate to numbers, quantities, capacity, weight, place of origin, mode of manufacture, package content, patents, fitness for purpose, conformity to standards, identity of supplier, and standing or competence of the manufacturer. The false statement can be in a picture rather than words, such as a picture of the Swiss Alps on a box of Finnish cheese.

The correct price must be clearly displayed, including extras such as installation or service charges, and one must not use top of the range models to give the impression that cheaper models have similar attributes. Displayed prices must include VAT. 'Free gifts' accompanying the product cannot be recouped in a raised product price. Even false claims of price reductions where a previous price is crossed off are forbidden. The use of recommended prices is strictly controlled.

Owners of multiple stores must take care that price reductions apply to every unit in a chain across a country.

While services providers, who do not supply products, can escape product liability, they are very much under the scrutiny of the consumer legislation. Typical services at risk range from hotels and travel agents to hairdressers, dry cleaners, accountants, lawyers and doctors, and the statements to avoid are any which might in any way not be exactly correct and will be found relating to the nature, effect or fitness for purpose of the service, and the time, place, manner or person by which the service is provided. Advertisements must be scrutinized carefully, particularly those with expressions such as no job too large or small, 24 hours a day service, and so on.

The misleading information has to be of a material nature, relating to false or misleading indications given knowingly or recklessly. The last is not likely if the person making it believes it to be true. If a careless statement about a future holiday resort was believed to be true at the time it was made, subsequent changes to the facts will not constitute recklessness.

Even advertising agencies, who knowingly publish advertisements which contain false or misleading information, can be liable, particularly where they are involved in designing campaigns and specific advertisements which use such information. Liability can also extend to certain publishers, such as newspapers and auctioneers. Price reductions in multiple stores must apply to every unit in a chain across and within a country.

A very important marketing and public relations matter for companies trading in Europe and in other markets where consumer rights legislation is strong is that more damage can accrue from the bad publicity that prosecutions can bring than from any fine, and that the power of the consumer has been hugely boosted by the existence of government consumer affairs or complaints departments, providing free services, and with powers of inspection and prosecution. The media love to expose companies who have the misfortune to transgress in matters of consumer protection. It makes for great so-called 'exposes', particularly in watchdog type television programmes which often dramatize and exaggerate the facts.

The products with specific regulations

How does a supplier ensure that products meet all the regulations which may be attached to them? In the first instance by knowing what categories of product attract a regulation and then ensuring that the manufacturer supplies them suitably marked as meeting the standard which attests to their compliance. Mostly this is a standard such as a BS or an ISO standard, but sometimes it is a 'mark' which demonstrates that groups of requirements are met, such as the famous BSI kitemark, or the EU CE Mark.

One cannot give a complete list of categories likely to attract legislation for all countries, but the following list may make a good beginning.

Typical consumer and product areas covered by regulations are:

- flammability of children's nightclothes
- toxicity and cellulosic content of children's toys
- ventilation of caravans and mobile homes
- safety of perambulators and pushchairs
- requirements for smoulder and flame resistant upholstery
- babies' soothers
- safety requirements for children's cots
- toxicity of pencils and graphic instruments
- rewirable 13 amp plugs
- safety of electrical equipment
- safety of workplace equipment
- anorak hood cords (covering the strength of hood cords in the anoraks of children under ten to prevent strangulation on swings and other apparatus)

- telecom equipment
- machinery
- personal protective equipment
- construction products
- medical equipment and drugs
- specialist areas where public safety is critical – aerospace, airline, medical, nuclear, many process industries
- food
- vehicles
- transport
- hotels and hospitality
- renting accommodation.

From time to time separate orders or statutory instruments will ban undesirable products, such as children's erasers and other devices which may be manufactured to look, smell and taste like candy or sweets.

The CE Mark in the EU assures buyers that all the regulations, including those for all the components within the product, have been met. Products requiring the EU CE Mark could also pose risks for retailers and installers within the EU, unless they are aware of the requirements.

All machinery dealers and services companies installing machinery in the EU must now take account of the Machinery Directive, which lists large fines and threats of imprisonment against individual managers amongst its almost repressive list of sanctions. Similar legislation is appearing elsewhere. The next few paragraphs are somewhat complex and may be of interest only to machinery dealers and installers, however a glance at them by other readers may give some indication of the extent to which regulations now affect services companies.

Since 1 January 1995 it has not been permissible for machinery which does not conform to the requirements of the directive to be sold in the European market. The Machinery Directive covers almost all machinery, with the exception of certain rare categories. The Directive also applies to safety components placed on the market separately.

'Machinery' is defined as an assembly of linked parts, at least one of which moves, for a specific application. 'Machinery' also applies to an assembly of machines which function as an integral whole, and also to interchangeable equipment which modifies the function of a machine.

'Safety component' is defined as a component which fulfils a safety function when in use, the failure or modification of which endangers the safety or health of exposed persons.

There has been confusion about who is responsible for meeting the requirements of the directive. Is the manufacturer/supplier only responsible or the plant user/owner? The answer is always the first, but it can be the second also.

Throughout the legislation one sees reference to the manufacturer, supplier and the one who puts the equipment into service. The last can be either the supplier or the new owner/user. The user may manufacture own machinery or parts thereof, thus being solely responsible for the units manufactured; the user may purchase from outside the EU, thus becoming the effective importer and 'putter into service' of the machinery, or the supplier may put it into service.

The manufacturer, or the importer of the machinery into Europe, or the one putting it into service is responsible for ensuring that the product conforms to the requirements of the Machinery Directive, which is that before placing the product on the market, the responsible person must:

(a) draw up a technical file
(b) if the machine or safety component is one of those listed under Annex IV of the Directive, submit the product to a notified body, for type-examination, (an approved test house), or if the product is manufactured in accordance with agreed standards, submit the technical file for verification by the notified body.
(c) draw up an EC Declaration of Conformity
(d) for machines only – affix the CE Mark (see below).

The technical file consists of:

- a complete drawing of the machine and control circuits, detailed drawings, calculation notes, test results, health and safety requirements
- a list of the essential requirements of the Directive, standards, and other technical specifications which were used when the machinery was designed
- a description of methods adopted to eliminate hazards presented by the machinery
- if so desired, any technical report or certificate obtained from a competent body or laboratory

- if conformity is declared with a harmonized standard which applies to the machinery, any technical report giving the results of tests carried out at the manufacturer's choice either by himself or by an appropriately accredited laboratory
- a copy of the instruction for the machinery.

7

The
Environmental
Management
System

The difference between ISO 9000 and ISO 14000

You can produce a 'quality' product to ISO 9000, a beautiful crystal decanter, say, and do it in a dirty and dangerous manner. ISO 9000 deals mainly with the control of the steps of production or services in the main product or service areas, while ISO 14000 deals with the *issues* in the environment affected by manufacturing or service operations, including product or service design, processing, end use and ultimate disposal, including waste caused by packaging. ISO 14000 also has additional legal significance as it allows control of health and safety, public safety and product/service safety, and also control of emergency and accident prevention procedures. Health and safety as a single subject is dealt with in the following chapter.

While a manufacturer can produce a quality product in a dirty and dangerous manner, it is difficult to find a quality service which can be delivered in a dirty or unhygienic or dangerous way, although you could have services perceived to be quality at the point of delivery which have bad environmental backgrounds and consequences. Hotels and restaurants cannot easily provide quality services which are environmentally unsound, although several leisure services could be environmentally unsound, such as golf courses, and speedboat and jet sky type water sports. In general it is more difficult to deliver a quality service which is environmentally unsound than it is to produce a quality product which wastes resources and causes pollution.

It is also much easier to implement a quality management system, to a standard such as ISO 9000, in a services company, which incorporates environmental and safety controls, whereas in manufacturing much of what is demanded by these two issues requires separate systems. Take a service station for example. On the main task of performing a quality service for customers, one needs merely to add a small number of controls for such 'environmental' issues (environmental used in the broadest sense) as the safe transfer of petroleum from tanker to storage tanks, controls on smoking at the pumps, and any needed hygiene controls for food sold in the forecourt stores or shops.

While there are as we have seen a small number of legal issues such as product liability managed under ISO 9000, nearly all of the environmental and health and safety issues managed under an environmental management system, such as ISO 14000, are compliance-driven, that is backed by the law. Many carry the potential for individual as well as corporate liability, some such as worker health and safety and the EU Machinery Directive even with a potential for jail sentences for individual managers. So apart from the excellent public relations and marketing appeal of introducing an environmental management system into your services business, there is the added attraction of the confidence that you have covered yourself against charges of negligence and opportunistic claims for compensation.

Who will be affected by the standard?

ISO 14000, the environmental management standard, is already following the course of ISO 9000 and affecting manufacturing industry first. As the major manufacturers adopt it, their suppliers of raw materials, components and print and packaging quickly follow, in the same kind of 'cascade' spread we saw with ISO 9000. Even before the standard was published in April 1992, in its earlier BSI form, BS 7750 (upon which ISO 14000 is based), the demands for demonstration of environmental consideration were increasing on manufacturers. Many service industries such as transport, power and mass retail outlets using packaging were also under pressure. The standard will eventually reach all sectors of manufacturing and services.

All those companies currently affected by environmental legislation and regulations, whether they concern air, water, waste, noise, product use, safety, or materials employed, will be affected by the standard. The new standard will help such companies to control their operations, maintain them within the regulations and demonstrate conformance with those regulations.

The demands for the standard come from the same direction as those for ISO 9000. To begin with, environmentally conscious buyers, both government and private, demand it, followed by large high street retailers, who want a green image. Manufacturers will, by necessity, have to force it downward on to their suppliers. Once the first companies become certified and start to promote their premier status, others will be forced for marketing reasons to follow. This has been the pattern for ISO 9000 and it will be the pattern for ISO 14000.

The general environmental issues

As we have seen in Chapter 4 which looked at the regulations, most of the environmental issues are covered by legislation. Each services company needs to look at the following list of general issues and ask if it is involved with any of them. If so, there will be a requirement under the law to deal with that issue. The general environmental issues which can be covered by both regulations and the ISO 14000 standard are:

- planning and environmental impact assessment
- emissions to the air
- discharges to water resources
- water supplies and sewage treatment
- waste

- nuisances
- noise
- odour
- radiation
- amenity, trees and wildlife
- urban renewal
- process/public safety
- packaging
- materials use
- energy use
- staff health and safety.

These can be summarized as: traditional environmental (emissions, discharges, wastes); staff health and safety; and public safety.

Within each company these will be further defined into specific operational issues, such as exposure to chemicals, risk of fire, control of water-based waste, control of emissions, toxic waste, and so on.

Let us look at the likelihood of some or all of these applying to your service.

Planning and environmental impact assessment

Planning permission will be required if you are planning a new facility or an extension of any kind in countries where planning permission legislation is in force. In most of these countries also, projects over a certain threshold value require a comprehensive environmental impact assessment, before the project can begin.

Emissions to the air

For most services companies it is unlikely that they would ever achieve a level of emissions to the air which warrants licensing from a local authority, and most unlikely that if they reached such levels they would ever exceed them. This is an issue for chemical and other process plants. Power stations could be big emissions offenders, unless they take preventative scrubbing actions.

Discharges to water resources

Increasingly legislation applies to service operations. In general there are two broad categories of drain – the storm drain and the foul drain. For decades businesses have been discharging waste water or water-based wastes down both. There is now legislation covering a number of types of waste which may or may not, either at all or in certain quantities, go down these drains.

Amongst the services which need to look at their discharges to water resources are hotels, large restaurants, service stations, garages, engineering repair shops, waste management operators, and any service which causes effluent to enter either its internal foul or sewer system or the outside storm (or rain) drains. Services which will find this a big issue are airports, transport companies, power stations.

Water supplies and sewage treatment

The supply of water and treatment of sewage can be issues for big hotels, managers of resorts, theme parks, passenger shipping companies, and of course they are of primary concern to local authorities, water supply and sewage treatment companies. Most small services depending on local authorities for these will find that they are not issues which they have to manage.

Waste

Waste is an issue for all companies, manufacturing and services.

All categories of waste are now covered by legislation, some more stringent than others. Unless the waste output is so small that it can be legally placed outside for pick up by municipal or local waste collectors, it will fall into some special category. These may be as follows:

- normal waste in such high volume that it requires a private licensed transporter, whose licence you should inspect at least once a year
- glass which should go to a recycling bank
- oil which should be removed by a licensed waste oil recovery company, whose licence you should inspect at least once a year
- timber, such as palettes, which should go to a timber recycler, not

mandatory in most countries but a good environmental practice
- crushed cans, which should go to a can recycler or can bank, not mandatory in most countries but a good environmental practice
- waste food, the legislation for which differs country to country but can be a highly regulated issue, requiring specialist disposal or recycling as animal feed
- hospital waste, which is both highly regulated and emotive, requiring incineration, itself a highly emotive issue
- precious metals from dental or gold or silver or similar services, the market value of which attracts recyclers
- toxic waste, which is highly regulated and which requires specialist licensed waste removers, whose licence you should inspect at least once a year.

Nuisances

Noise is covered below, but legislation is emerging in Europe and elsewhere covering a range of nuisance-type activities, including noise, such as unsightly sites, pools of water, behaviour of patrons, and so on. This needs examination by hotels, fun fairs, bars, discos, night spots, and the likes.

Noise

Noise is now a big issue in large process plants, particularly chemicals and food. Both internal worker and outside 'fenceline' decibel level rules apply, and relate to the kinds of ear protection required and to upper limits. Services involved with noise, in particular discos, face not only legislation, but risk the possibility of large compensation claims from both real injured customers and the opportunistic, if a recorded decibel level reading, admissible in court as expert evidence, shows that permitted levels are, or were, exceeded. Neighbours now also have legislated rights to protection from noise from each other in many countries.

Odour

Odour is another problem for chemical and food process companies. While it is difficult to see how any service company could stay in business if it has an odour problem, some reader somewhere may know of such a strange thing.

Radiation

Radiation is an important issue for hospitals and laboratories, but so regulated that anyone involved will know the regulations and standards. It is, however, a potentially critical issue for management, fraught with danger for companies which might be negligent.

Amenity, trees and wildlife

The natural environment used to be an issue for manufacturers and airports only, but increasingly affects other service companies. Golf clubs, outdoor leisure centres and theme parks are now under official and private scrutiny, while no one needs reminding of what is happening in blood sports. It seems likely that both regulations and public reaction against abuses of landscape and wildlife will increase.

Urban renewal

Most service operators will have the good sense to know that they must respect listed buildings and urban renewal schemes and not either maintain derelict sites or cause them to become derelict, as this area invites bad press as well as prosecution.

Process/public safety

Process/public safety is a fundamental issue for transport companies and hospitals, as well as indoor and outdoor leisure activities. New EU legislation for fun fairs is an indication of the increasing regulations in this area. It is critical that operators in these services know the specialized regulations which apply to them and inconceivable that they would be in business without this being the case.

Packaging/waste/litter

While packaging in the first instance is the responsibility of the manufacturer, the service providing the package across the counter is being asked to assist in its return or recycling to reduce packaging waste and to avoid litter – witness the frantic efforts of well-known fast food chains to stop customers throwing away burger wrappers and soft drinks cups, and the EU packaging waste directive making suppliers take back the waste packaging.

Materials use

There is an environmental rather than legal, requirement for all companies to reduce in-house materials usage, from copy paper to internal envelopes. While you will not break the law by ignoring it, you will save money, often substantially.

Energy use

This is also environmentally rather than legally driven, more visible than in-house materials usage, and it has become almost a moral issue where energy wasters are bad people. It also makes a lot of sense being a potentially big money saving area.

Staff health and safety

The issue of staff health and safety is such a critical one for services companies that Chapter 8 is entirely devoted to it.

ISO 14 000 – the environmental management standard

ISO 14000 is the world's first agreed environmental management standard, based on an existing BSI standard. The environmental management standard specifies the requirements for implementing and maintaining an environmental management system which can also demonstrate that it complies with company environmental policy and complies with the relevant regulations.

In practice what this means is that a company must document the evidence that it is aware of regulations, and build a management system which can ensure compliance with those regulations, and finally produce evidence of that system for inspection.

A summary of what is involved

The first steps after achieving management commitment are to carry out an initial environmental review and construct a register of regulations with the actual relevant statutory instruments (acts of parliament) inside, usually in plastic see-through envelopes in ring binders. Using the initial environmental review and the Register of Regulations, one establishes the issues of relevance; the rest of the job is specifying these as exactly as possible, projecting limits to be maintained and designing and documenting controls. The two main assurance elements of the standard are assurance to oneself that one is in compliance with a stated environmental policy, and a demonstration of that compliance to others, the latter normally achieved through certification.

ISO 14000, and the environmental management system it represents, are being embraced by companies looking for a target beyond the 'quality' of ISO 9000 and by those already under pressure to produce evidence of environmental care. It is valuable to companies who want to use it to give them a market and PR advantage, particularly in Europe, the US, and other sophisticated markets. It will be particularly relevant for those selling into the EU public procurement market, for those selling to demanding buyers, and for those marketing products and services that are enhanced by environmental accreditation.

Seeing the strength of consumer protection and misleading advertising legislation, it is reasonable that false claims of environmental friendliness will soon be proscribed, so that the words 'environmentally friendly' will not remain as demeaned as 'quality' was before the advent of ISO 9000.

There is a great deal of interest in ISO 14000 in Europe, the US and Canada, and many companies in the UK have anticipated it by implementing BS 7750 systems. Companies which have achieved ISO 9000 are finding the new environment standard easier to implement than those which have not; at the same time it is possible to go for ISO 14000 first, but whether one should do that depends on pressures from buyers. If buyers are demanding ISO 9000 first, then ISO 9000 is the only sensible route to the ultimate standard of both.

A services company which wants to fully implement an ISO 14000 system should consult the *ISO 14000 and ISO 9000* (Rothery, 1995).

8

Health and Safety

Health and safety may be the area most needing attention for services companies large or small, and a dangerous area for small companies who, through lack of awareness, are more likely to neglect their demanding requirements. In particular in Europe and North America, and in most countries in the developed world, there now exist stringent regulations covering staff health and safety, which carry both dangers of fines and imprisonment for individual owners and managers. It is no exaggeration to say that one is indeed in more danger of breaking the law here as an honest trader than is a careful criminal. There is the added danger here that prosecutions for neglecting regulations could lead to opportunistic claims for compensation from alliances between staff members and unscrupulous solicitors or lawyers.

The recipe for staying safe, already shown in the chapters on the fast track (Chapter 2) and full systems (Chapter 3), states the simple rules –

'know the law, write the procedures, train the staff, implement the controls'. The most practical way to ensure that this is done is to incorporate the health and safety regulations under a quality/ environmental management system, so that each of them is controlled automatically as if it were any other issue, such as waste or quality of service.

Only in the countries of the EU are the health and safety regulations almost fully harmonized, making it easy to identify them, read their requirements and put a management or control system in place. It is one of the most standardized areas of European regulations, the reason being that the European Commission has written explicit directives on each of the specific worker health and safety issues and, as each such directive is published, the member states adopt it with little or no change, and make it law through the issuance of national statutory instruments.

Knowing the law

As with all of the regulations, the difficult task of trying to know the law and stay up to date on it must be undertaken. What is at stake is avoiding a situation where a company or an individual manager can be prosecuted for negligence. The negligence can arise only if a regulation and its necessary controls are ignored. The negligence could come to light either through an inspection from a national health and safety executive inspector, or as a result of a court action brought by an injured staff member whose lawyer has noticed the shortcoming.

There are key sources of information on the health and safety regulations in most western countries. Every EU office in Europe will make available the EU health and safety regulations; in addition, most if not all European countries have a national health and safety authority or executive which issues free lists of the regulations and guides to their implementation. One important central source of information in the US is the Department of Energy (DOE) which publishes the health and safety regulations. The DOE also has an excellent site on the Internet which gives full details of the regulations. Information both at federal and state level on the regulations is also available from Cornel University, which also has an excellent Internet site.

Industry associations have been slow to realise the need for a regulation identification and updating service for their members, and companies should put pressure on them to earn their fees to do this for all regulations, trading, environmental and health and safety. This author has had the frustrating experience of writing about this for at least three years with little effect to be seen from either industry associations or chambers of commerce. Companies are not being served well either in the business of knowing the regulations or achieving certification to ISO 9000 or ISO 14000.

Building the system

Purchase the actual health and safety regulations and insert them into plastic see-through envelopes as part of the ring binder which acts as the Register of Regulations, or include them as part two of the register in a second ring binder. If you can afford to do so, use a specialist consultant to do this and all the other document creation in your overall quality/environmental/health and safety system. Alternatively purchase a package which helps you do this from a publisher such as Gower.

Treat the health and safety regulations within the system as any other quality or environmental issue for control and auditing purposes.

As they are legislated for separately, and under scrutiny from health and safety inspectors who may know little or nothing about environmental management matters, put all the specific health and safety procedures into a separate Health and Safety Manual, with related and cross-referenced standard operating procedures. This manual should include a policy statement which also meets the statutory requirement of what is called a 'safety statement' demanded by the legislation.

Devise a separate staff health and safety training course.

The Health and Safety Manual

What now follows is a sample outline of a comprehensive Health and Safety Manual for a service company. It also incorporates public safety, which may be relevant only to certain companies and probably most large services companies, such as those operating extensive facilities with emergency response considerations, which could involve customers, staff and the local community.

Sample Health and Safety Manual

Table of contents

Part 1   Administration

1   How to use this manual
2   What the law demands
3   Place of health and safety manual in overall procedures
4   Policy including Safety statement
5   Organization and responsibilities
6   Staff consultation and co-operation

Part 2   Safety procedures

1   Workplace
2   Equipment
3   Personal protective equipment
4   Manual handling
5   VDUs
6   Electrical
7   First aid
8   Exposure to carcinogens
9   Exposure to noise
10   Handling of dangerous substances
11   Safety signs
12   Pregnant workers
13   Notification of accidents
14   Task analysis
15   Fork lift trucks
16   Batteries
17   Confined spaces
18   Hot work
19   LPG (liquid petroleum gas)
20   Compressed air
21   Steam/pressure vessels
22   Contractors/visitors/customers on site
23   Other (as required)

Part 3   Occupational health

1   Medical services
2   Eye and audiometric tests

3 Resources available/welfare

4 Training programmes

Part 4 Loss control

1 Audits and reviews

2 Emergency response

3 Accident procedures

4 Security

5 The management controls

6 Standards used

This is a typical list of the Standard Operating Procedures or SOPs, which is by no means complete:

List of SOPs

SOP

1 Emergency and evacuation procedures manual

2 Permits to work

3 Safe workplace

4 Noise

5 Safe equipment

6 Personal protective equipment

7 Manual handling

8 VDUs

9 Fork lift trucks

10 Handling of dangerous substances

11 Working in confined spaces

12 Hot work

13 Safety signs

14 Pregnant workers

15 Batteries

16 Compressed air

17 Steam boilers/pressure vessels

18 Contractors/visitors

19 Office

20 Electricity

21 Electrical power tools

22 Compressed air power tools

23 Automatic doors

24 Workshops

25 Window cleaning

26 Work at heights/fragile roofs

27 Ladders

28 Step ladders/trestles/staging

29 Loading bay/truck movements

30 Trucks

31 Exposure to carcinogens

32 LPG (liquid petroleum gas)

33 Welding

34 Internal vehicles

35 Scaffolding

36 Mobile towers

Sample health and safety regulations – using the EU as a model

The regulations which are made into local law by each country cover the following areas:

- general health and safety (under the Framework and Safety, Health and Welfare at Work Regulation)
- workplace
- work equipment
- visual display units
- manual handling
- personal protective equipment
- pregnant workers
- temporary workers
- safety signs
- limit values
- asbestos worker protection
- carcinogens
- biological agents
- exposure to noise
- first aid
- electricity
- notification of accidents and dangerous occurrences.

Also on the way are directives for working hours (under dispute in the EU), young people at work, mines and quarries, offshore, vessels, transport of dangerous goods, exposure to dangerous substances, activities in the transport sector, fairgrounds and playgrounds.

This list must not be taken as complete and may also be further added to by the time this book is published. Only a list obtained from your local EU or health and safety office can ensure that you know what the full regulations are.

9

Who Needs Standards?

Businesses needing the quality management standard

Badly needing it for the sake of the suffering customer

The paragraphs that follow could be considered wishful thinking as the worst offenders do not have to answer to anyone. A state body or a world-famous tourist site might be able to afford to treat customers as nuisances or supplicants, in the short term at least. Generally those who treat their customers as supplicants are either impregnable fortresses, such as departments of inland revenue, or have their days numbered.

In the case of a popular tourist resort, such as a world-famous shrine, giving bad service, national interests eventually recognize that bad service from even the most popular resort can damage the rest of a country's tourist industry.

In the case of the incompetent state body, it may simply become so bad that competition and deregulation are introduced to erode its monopolistic mandates.

Badly needing it because the customer demands it

Businesses which increasingly require standards because the customer demands it include:

- all those companies selling a service, no matter what service, into large sophisticated companies, in particular into manufacturers or major service companies
- all those companies selling a service which involves stringent quality requirements
- all those companies selling a service into a highly regulated area – hospitals, supermarkets, restaurants, airlines, and so on.

Here is a list of services provided to its sophisticated customers, which Merchant Gardner, the huge contract catering company, kindly supplied.

- cleaning (general and specialist)
- porterage
- courier
- building fabric maintenance
- mechanical and electrical maintenance
- catering
- bar management
- vending
- housekeeping
- secretarial
- security
- gardening and landscaping
- snow clearing
- purchasing and procurement
- transport management
- waste disposal
- provision of workwear

- reception
- mail/messenger
- conference administration
- reprographic/office equipment
- archives and storage
- microfilming
- library
- telecom/fax/telex
- car park management
- swimming pool management
- medical/first aid support
- health and safety support
- road cleaning/repair
- temporary accommodation
- space utilization/planning
- travel administration
- pest control
- asset registration/control
- project planning
- indoor planters/maintenance
- leisure centre management
- creche management
- general refurbishment
- planned maintenance systems
- structural adaptations
- architectural consultancy
- quantity surveying
- civil/structural/mechanical and electrical consultancy
- training centre management.

If you are a service company providing any of these services to local divisions of foreign owned companies or multinational companies or to large national companies, you may already have been asked to adopt ISO 9000, or may shortly be asked to do so. This requirement, unfortunately perhaps for some small companies, may come on top of one other requirement – that of being required under the new outsourcing practices to provide many or all services in a range of services, as buyers place more and more business with fewer suppliers, and in many cases all business of the same or related kinds with one supplier. For more information on this subject see *The Truth about Outsourcing* (Rothery and Robertson, 1995). On top of this pincer movement of demand for quality system certification and catering for all categories in a service line is the other exterior and also growing demand of increasing regulation from the state.

Badly needing it but don't know what they are doing wrong

In the absence of what engineers may call 'negative feedback', which lets one know what is wrong, an absence caused by no one telling a company about its bad service, a company may slide downwards in ignorance of the reasons.

Examples include telephones not answered, or callers left holding, calls not returned, excuses such as 'We can't move you on that day, or any other day that week, because we are moving Coopers and Lybrand, all ten floors for them, and they are just one of our corporate clients.' Meaning that you are a mere member of the public wanting to move house and, as we have customers such as Coopers and Lybrand, we are too busy to handle the likes of you. Here we are rejected supplicants, but what the service refuser does not realise is that he or she is not doing any favours for their corporate customers either.

There is the all too common restaurant where staff seldom or never get the courses right. We would like the sherry first, soup next, glass of wine with main course, tartar sauce with the fish without having to get up to ask for it – all both satisfying to us and less time consuming and costly and annoying than getting this order of events wrong, but how often do they happen in that right order? Quality service is getting it right first time.

Pop and rock music or radio stations playing in supermarkets or convenience stores, and not just playing but blasting forth. The staff may be young and feel that they have a right to express their culture, and that the problem is not with them but with those too old to appreciate it who are no longer of this world. The problem for the store owners is that these old people may have 'deep pockets', the contents of which they will transfer to stores where there is no loud pop music.

Worse than the stores playing pop music is the radio station manned by a disc jockey, or broadcasting advertisements, while one is eating in a restaurant. Customers will stop using such restaurants and may never tell the proprietors that it was because of its radio playing policy, or, worse still, the large television screen switched on in the hotel lunch bar.

There is the frustrating run around in the book store from Billy to Julie and back to Billy. Billy informs you that if the book is not with the wholesalers you will have to wait three weeks. You give the order anyway and as he keys it in he goes on talking to a woman colleague, who at one stage during your wait asks him, 'How did you sleep last night?' In this specific incident, the supplicant customer told this author that she felt that she was irrelevant.

Finally, in this category, there is the almost incredible response to the telephone enquiry, along the lines of 'You will have to talk with the boss when he comes in, whenever that might be.' This person sometimes appears surprised that the telephone has actually rung or that a caller wants to discuss possible business. There may be no attempt to offer to take a name or call back. When the supplicant hangs up it will be final.

Businesses needing the environmental management standard

Let us look at the services companies who are working towards it first:

- hotels
- large computer and software suppliers
- service stations
- transport companies
- print and packaging companies.

Who will be affected by the standard?

Chapter 7 has covered this question in some detail, but in general services companies are only now following manufacturers in implementing quality management, or ISO 9000, systems. As Chapter 7 points out, however, many services companies will be attracted to the legal assurances which can be provided by ISO 14000.

Businesses needing certification to either or both standards

It is important to distinguish between implementing a quality and environmental management standard and having it certified. Any one of us can adopt ISO 9000 and ISO 14000 and claim that we are operating to the standards. Only when a large buyer whom we need to keep happy demands certification do we have to submit our systems and our businesses to the inspection of a certification agency to obtain the piece of paper which demonstrates compliance with the standards. One other reason why we might regard certification as a necessity is when we want to ensure that should we ever have to stand up in court and defend ourselves against charges of negligence or opportunistic claims for compensation, we will have the best independent third-party corroboration that we have employed 'a best code of practice'.

Many people refer to 'ISO certification'. There is no ISO certification, and it is to be hoped that ISO remains independent of certification schemes, which for now at least are carried out by independent organizations who are themselves subjected to accreditation usually by a single, often state-owned, body within each country.

Against the benefits offered by ISO 9000 and ISO 14000 implementation, certification may offer a threat. Certification is open to abuse by over-zealous inspectors, it confers police-type powers on to petty officials, and it can become a barrier to enterprise to small companies and single traders.

PART II

The Quality Management Documentation

Introduction

To get as much value as possible from this Part the reader should study two figures, the first one below and the second on page 126, which explain the documentation required for the implementation of ISO 9000 and ISO 14000 systems, with ISO 14000 managing health and safety also, and the specific documentation needed by service sector category.

The ISO 9000 documentation for quality management

The figure on page 78 explains what is required.

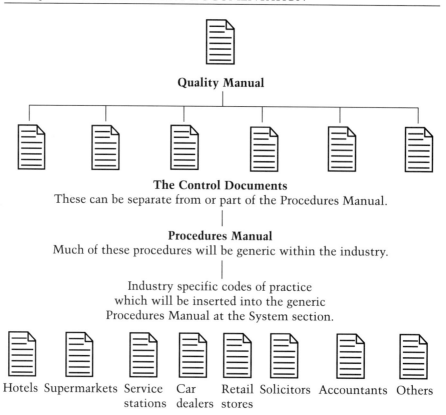

Quality Manual

The Control Documents
These can be separate from or part of the Procedures Manual.

Procedures Manual
Much of these procedures will be generic within the industry.

Industry specific codes of practice
which will be inserted into the generic
Procedures Manual at the System section.

Hotels Supermarkets Service Car Retail Solicitors Accountants Others
stations dealers stores

Here will be the specific procedures for the service sector.

The Quality Manual

There are three levels of documentation needed in ISO 9000, and they are often referred to as Level 1, Level 2 and Level 3.

The top level is the Quality Manual, a sample outline of which is shown on pages 81–83.

The next level is made up of all the specific documents needed to control the issues which are fundamental to quality. Examples include: quality plans, measurement and testing routines, inspection and test records, customer specifications, customer performance, supplier/vendor specifications, sales order processing procedure.

The third and lowest level is made up of the standard operating procedures, known as the SOPs. Please note that there can be variations of this – for example control documents at the second level, or a further level of simple instructions at the shop floor or counter level with full procedures in the offices.

In summary we have a Quality Manual which breaks down into detailed operating procedures and, in whatever form is practical, single or multiple sheets of instructions if necessary at operator stations, with control documents in the office. As the last two are company specific, we can deal only in some depth with two here – the Quality Manual and the operating procedures. Even in these two cases we can look only at the table of contents level for space reasons. Readers who want full packages of generic documentation which they can customize to their own operations should contact the publisher Gower, or look under 'ISO 9000 or ISO 14000 documentation' on the Internet.

Document index

The documents below are a mixture of control records and procedures/instructions. The intention is to show you how such documents must back up the Quality Manual and be referenced to it. Where reference is made to a procedure, such as non-conforming procedures, these procedures also contain records, such as non-conforming material, or non-conforming component.

List of documents involved

(This is repeated in the Quality Manual as a document index.)

This is to demonstrate that while the Quality Manual is the most important document, many other documents, the masters of which can be in the Quality Manual, are also needed. The ones now shown are simply representative as your own procedures determine your documentation needs.

DC-01	Document master list
DC-02	Amendment list
DC-03	Circulation list
DC-04	Organization chart
QM-01	Quality Manual
QP-01	Quality plans (overview of inspection, test, audit and review procedures)
MT-01	Measurement and testing routines
IT-01	Inspection and test records

CS-01	Customers' specifications
CP-01	Customer performance
SP-01	Suppliers/vendor specifications
SP-02	Supplier/purchasing procedures
SP-03	Approved vendor list
SO-01	Sales order processing procedure
CCR-01	Records of contract reviews
DP-01	Design procedures
PDP-01	Product design and development plan
PC-01	Product catalogues
PS-01	Product specification
QF-01	Quote file
SP-01	Safety procedures
SOP-01	Operating procedures
SOP-02	Continued
-03	Continued
-09	Continued
SOP-00	Special process procedures
IN-01	Inspection procedures, including goods inwards, goods inward inspection (GII) and In-process Inspection and Testing Procedure (these can be in the operating procedures)
ST-01	Stores procedures
QP-01	Non-conforming procedures
QP-02	Corrective action procedure
QP-03	Non-conforming product review and disposition procedure

Important note

The above are sample documents only, given as a representative example of what are needed. Your own documents and procedures will be determined by the services, products and processes employed, as well as by your house style and existing documentation regime. Large companies will need more documents, small ones less. Some companies may need only a few of the documents listed.

For control purposes, however, four basic elements are needed and these are – what is the job/control, who is doing it, what is the status and when was it done?

These should be reflected in control documents which have such headings as:

Job	Check employed	Operator initials	Date

Other important control documents will simply reflect the overall status of inspections and checks, acting as logs.

Sample Quality Manual contents

Section	Clause	Subject
0.1	---	Circulation list
0.2	---	Amendment list
0.3	---	Table of contents
0.4	---	Scope and field of application
0.5	---	Document index
0.6	---	Amendment procedure
0.7	---	Description of company
1.0	4.1	Management responsibility
		Quality policy
		Organization
		Management review
2.0	4.2	Quality system procedures
3.0	4.3	Contract review
4.0	4.4	Design control
		General
		Design and development planning
		Design input
		Design output
		Design verification and validation
		Design changes

5.0	4.5	Document and data control
		Document approval and issue
		Document changes/modifications
6.0	4.6	Purchasing
		General
		Assessment of sub-contractors
		Purchasing data
		Verification of purchased products
7.0	4.7	Control of customer-supplied product
8.0	4.8	Product identification and traceability
9.0	4.9	Process control
		General
		Special processes
10.0	4.10	Inspection and testing
		Receiving inspection and testing
		In-process inspection and testing
		Final inspection and testing
		Inspection and test records
11.0	4.11	Inspection, measuring, and test equipment
12.0	4.12	Inspection and test status
13.0	4.13	Control of non-conforming product
		Non-conformity review and disposition
14.0	4.14	Corrective and preventative action
15.0	4.15	Handling, storage, packaging, preservation and delivery
		General
		Handling
		Storage
		Packaging
		Delivery

16.0	4.16	Quality records
17.0	4.17	Internal quality audits
18.0	4.18	Training
19.0	4.19	Servicing
20.0	4.20	Statistical techniques

See Appendix I for a sample quality procedures manual.

Sectoral Codes of
Practice for
ISO 9000

Important note

The services codes of practice which follow are in some cases supplied by large services companies and in others partly designed by this author. They appear here in advance of standards which will be developed by ISO technical committees, and, thus, like much else written by this author on standards, are one person's vision of what might constitute good codes of practice, or at least make a basis for them. Because of immense difficulties experienced by this author and others over recent years to find any kind of consensus on agreed codes of practice, and because of ISO technical committees' obscure pronouncements on the matter, an attempt is now being made to set up an international benchmarking scheme, controlled by industry, through which companies will share and agree benchmarks for specific sectoral codes of practice. Readers wanting to know more about this should access the Internet site at http://ireland.iol.ie/rothery and, in case of changes after the publication of this book, search on a search engine such as Infoseek under 'ISO 14000 documentation'.

The reader should fully appreciate that what follows may not be either the best or the only codes of practice, and that only a search within one's own industry or through an industry association may reveal what may be a good or 'best' code, if there is such a thing.

It may help the reader considerably to know in advance where these codes fit into an overall system. A study of figures on pages 78 and 126, together with the system shown below for retail stores should be studied to appreciate this. The retail store system can be regarded as a generic model for all services with variations only for banks, supermarkets, solicitors and others.

Furthermore, all these codes are in a state of evolution, and even ISO is only now beginning to set up the technical committees which, hopefully, will produce sectoral codes. Some are in the form of checklists while others are more developed in the form of summaries of procedures. The important point is not how well they are developed, or how standardized their presentation here, but how well they act as lists of the issues concerned, as fundamental to establishing services standards is knowing what issues to manage in the first instance. It is in this spirit that they are now being offered as they stand. If any reader is prepared to make more complete versions available for publication, this author will be grateful to receive them.

The services sectors addressed are as follows:

- hotels
- supermarkets
- service stations
- general dealerships
- chain and other retail stores
- solicitors and the legal profession
- accountants
- banks
- restaurants
- other.

Hotels

For help and advice with this section, this author is indebted to the Doyle Hotel Group and to the Jurys Hotel Group, the second of which appears to have been the world's first hotel group to have implemented ISO 9000 in the hotel industry.

It is in questionnaire or checklist form rather than procedures, but it identifies tasks or activities, or 'issues' requiring procedures.

Hotel Questionnaire

Form 1: The Service Characteristics

There are four distinct groups of services within the hotel business. These are:

A — Accommodation
B — Restaurant/Bar
C — Leisure Centre – Entertainment
D — Conference and Banqueting

Because of space limitations, only the first of these, Accommodation, is taken to the next level of detail.

Form 1A: The Service Characteristics – Accommodation

Elements

1A.1	Bedrooms
1A.2	Guest facilities
1A.3	Recreational facilities
1A.4	Capacity/accessibility
1A.5	Effective communication
1A.6	Reception/lobby
1A.7	Safety
1A.8	Personnel
1A.9	Comfort/aesthetics/maintenance

Form 1A.1 Bedrooms	
Elements	*Comments*
1A.1.1 Range 1A.1.2 Specifics 1A.1.3 Comfort/aesthetics 1A.1.4 Hygiene	

Form 1A.1.1 Range of bedrooms	
Elements	*Comments*
1A.1.1.1 Full suites 1A.1.1.2 Half suites 1A.1.1.3 Single rooms 1A.1.1.4 Double rooms 1A.1.1.5 Twin and family rooms 1A.1.1.6 Cots, foldaway beds	

Form 1A.1.2 Specifics of bedroom	
Elements	*Comments*
1A.1.2.1 Toilet 1A.1.2.2 Shower 1A.1.2.3 Bath 1A.1.2.4 Wash-hand basin 1A.1.2.5 Windows and curtains 1A.1.2.6 Bed/bedclothes/pillows/ mattresses/mattress covers 1A.1.2.7 Bedside table/locker 1A.1.2.8 Storage space 1A.1.2.9 Dressing table 1A.1.2.10 Wastepaper basket 1A.1.2.11 Telephone/TV 1A.1.2.12 Electrical outlets 1A.1.2.13 Sound proofing 1A.1.2.14 Lights 1A.1.2.15 Mirrors 1A.1.2.16 Stationery	

Form 1A.1.3 Comfort/Aesthetics (re Bedroom)	
Elements	*Comments*
1A.1.3.1 Heating/ventilation 1A.1.3.2 Lighting 1A.1.3.3 Extra lounge chairs 1A.1.3.4 Decor 1A.1.3.5 Mini bar 1A.1.3.6 Guest accessories i.e. soaps, shampoo etc, dressing gowns/slippers 1A.1.3.7 Room service 1A.1.3.8 Laundry facilities	

Form 1A.1.4 Hygiene – Bedroom	
Elements	*Comments*
1A.1.4.1 Daily cleaning of room 1A.1.4.2 Regular boil washing of towels 1A.1.4.3 Emptying & cleaning of waste paper baskets 1A.1.4.4 Change of bed linen 1A.1.4.5 Change of bed linen every three nights per stay 1A.1.4.6 Weekly cleaning 1A.1.4.7 Monthly, additional cleaning, e.g. skirting boards	

Form 1A.2 Guest Facilities	
Elements	*Comments*
1A.2.1 Child care 1A.2.2 Public telephone 1A.2.3 Laundry and service 1A.2.4 Room service 1A.2.5 Shop 1A.2.6 Postal service 1A.2.7 Safety boxes 1A.2.8 Credit card acceptability 1A.2.9 Beauty salon 1A.2.10 First aid stations 1A.2.11 Lost property	

Form 1A.3 Recreational Facilities	
Elements	*Comments*
1A.3.1 Swimming pool 1A.3.2 Golf course 1A.3.3 Children's play area 1A.3.4 Gym 1A.3.5 Jacuzzi 1A.3.6 Sauna 1A.3.7 Games room (pool, video games etc.) 1A.3.8 Discounts at facilities near hotel for patrons of hotel 1A.3.9 Availability*	

*i.e. facilities should be open at times suitable to all patrons – e.g. early enough for the business person to use comfortably before the working day begins.

Form 1A.4 Capacity/Accessibility	
Elements	*Comments*
1A.4.1 Disabled access 1A.4.2 Sufficient space in public areas 1A.4.3 Car park/entrance	

Form 1A.4.1 Disabled Access	
Elements	*Comments*
1A.4.1.1 Ramps/lifts/general accessibility in hotel 1A.4.1.2 Toilets 1A.4.1.3 Parking spaces near main door	

Form 1A.4.2 Car park/Entrance	
Elements	*Comments*
1A.4.2.1 Two lane entrance 1A.4.2.2 Pedestrian entrance 1A.4.2.3 Sufficient parking spaces 1A.4.2.4 Supervision 1A.4.2.5 Hotel staff using car park	

Form 1A.5 Effective Communication	
Elements	*Comments*
1A.5.1 Management/staff 1A.5.2 Management/patron 1A.5.3 Staff/patron	

Form 1A.5.1 Management/Staff Communication	
Elements	*Comments*
1A.5.1.1 Trade union 1A.5.1.2 Social club 1A.5.1.3 Regular meetings	

Form 1A.5.2 Management/Patron Communication	
Elements	*Comments*
1A.5.2.1 Direct contact with guests i.e. Management on the floor 1A.5.2.2 Complaints mechanism	

Form 1A.6 Reception/Lobby Area	
Elements	*Comments*
1A.6.1 Receptionist 1A.6.2 Porter's desk 1A.6.3 Sufficient desk space for reception and porter's desks 1A.6.4 Comfortable seating and reading material 1A.6.5 Waiting time/ Responsiveness 1A.6.6 Initial greeting	

Form 1A.6.1 Receptionist	
Elements	*Comments*
1A.6.1.1 Courteous 1A.6.1.2 Efficient 1A.6.1.3 Basic knowledge of languages 1A.6.1.4 Telephone skills 1A.6.1.5 Local knowledge 1A.6.1.5 Hotel knowledge	

Form 1A.7 Safety/Health	
Elements	*Comments*
1A.7.1 Workplace 1A.7.2 Work equipment 1A.7.3 Personal protective equipment 1A.7.4 Handling of loads 1A.7.5 Safety/health signs 1A.7.6 Safety and health of pregnant workers and workers who have recently given birth or are breast feeding 1A.7.7 Young people at work 1A.7.8 Exposure to carcinogens 1A.7.9 VDU 1A.7.10 Play area 1A.7.11 Working hours 1A.7.12 Handling-storing chemicals 1A.7.13 Safety shoes	

Form 1A.8 Personnel	
Elements	*Comments*

1A.8.1   Recruitment criteria
1A.8.2   Training – induction
1A.8.3   Facilities
1A.8.4   Procedural manuals/
          instructions
1A.8.5   Uniform
1A.8.6   Manager/senior on duty
          24 hours per day	

Form 1A.8.2 Training	
Elements	*Comments*

1A.8.2.1   Induction training
1A.8.2.2   Are the service and
           service delivery issues
           revealed here covered in
           the training manuals?
1A.8.2.3   Adequacy of specific
           training viz. hygiene
1A.8.2.4   Customer relations
1A.8.2.5   Competence/accuracy/
           completeness
1A.8.2.6   *Job specific training?*
       a.   Management/Senior
            staff
       b.   Receptionist
       c.   Doorman
       d.   Porter
       e.   Waiter
       f.   Bar staff
       g.   Car park attendant
       h.   Cooking staff
       i.   Cleaning staff
       j.   Child minders
       k.   Maintenance
       l.   Language training
       m. Hygiene
1A.6.2.7 Refresher courses	

Form 1A.8.3 Staff Facilities	
Elements	*Comments*
1A.8.3.1 Canteen 1A.8.3.2 Locker rooms 1A.8.3.3 Toilets 1A.8.3.4 Showers 1A.8.3.5 Social clubs 1A.8.3.6 Games room 1A.8.3.7 Live in accommodation	

Form 1A.8.5 Uniform	
Elements	*Comments*
1A.8.5.1 Practicality 1A.8.5.2 Smartness 1A.8.5.3 Tidiness 1A.8.5.4 Relevance to position 1A.8.5.5 Hygiene 1A.8.5.6 Staff i.d. badges	

Form 1A.9 Comfort/Aesthetics/Maintenance	
Elements	*Comments*
1A.9.1 Grounds 1A.9.2 Heating/ventilation 1A.9.3 Suitable lighting 1A.9.4 Seating in public areas 1A.9.5 Decor 1A.9.6 Paintings etc. on walls 1A.9.7 Floor covering 1A.9.8 Music in public areas	

Supermarkets

For help and advice with this section, this author is indebted to the Superquinn supermarket group.

Procedures which state policies, targets, and control limits, and all the necessary controls for these need to be written and in place covering the following service characteristics.

Section 1   The service characteristics as seen or experienced by the customer – (not those hidden from the customer dealt with later)

1   Capacity/accessibility
2   Personnel
3   Products/services
4   Waiting time/responsiveness
5   Hygiene/housekeeping
6   Safety (which can be managed under the health and safety system)
7   Courtesy
8   Comfort/aesthetics
9   State of the art technology
10   Effective communication
11   Range of services
12   Environmental probity/awareness (which can be managed under an environmental management system using ISO 14000 as a guide or the controlling mechanism)
13   An ISO 9000 quality management system (which may cover all of the quality issues here), as a guide or the controlling mechanism for service quality)

Samples only of the elements requiring control within some of these follow.

Form 1.1 Capacity/Accessibility		
Elements	*Yes/No*	*Comments*
1.1.1 Car park/entrance 1.1.2 Aisles 1.1.3 Shelf space 1.1.4 Yard 1.1.5 Disabled access	*	

*This can be a simple once-off check to ascertain if we have a car park and proper entrance. If we have these then the next form can apply.

Form 1.1.1 Car park/Entrance		
Elements	*Yes/No*	*Comments*
1.1.1.1 Used by local business people 1.1.1.2 Personnel using car park 1.1.1.3 Overcrowding 1.1.1.4 Obstruction of main road 1.1.1.5 Two lane entrance 1.1.1.6 Pedestrian entrance		

Form 1.1.2 Aisles		
Elements	*Yes/No*	*Comments*
1.1.2.1 Overcrowding 1.1.2.2 Lack of space during stocking 1.1.2.3 Width		

Form 1.2 Personnel		
Elements	*Yes/No*	*Comments*
1.2.1 Recruitment criteria 1.2.2 Training 1.2.3 Facilities 1.2.4 Security 1.2.5 Procedural manuals/ instructions 1.2.6 Uniform		

Form 1.3 Products/Services		
Elements	*Yes/No*	*Comments*
1.3.1 The product/service range 1.3.2 The quality/price suitability for the market being served 1.3.3 Correctness of shelf numbers/re-order levels 1.3.4 Re-order response times 1.3.5 Display		

Even in a product-oriented supermarket the range of services on offer can be very important (see Form 1.11 below).

Form 1.11 Range of Services		
Elements	*Yes/No*	*Comments*
1.11.1 Home delivery service 1.11.2 Local news/ announcements board 1.11.3 Umbrellas (if raining) for customers 1.11.4 Carrying heavy goods to customers cars if required 1.11.5 Made-to-order goods, e.g. cakes, hampers 1.11.6 Phone-in ordering 1.11.7 Creche/nappy changing facilities 1.11.8 Express checkouts 1.11.9 Credit 1.11.10 Knife sharpening 1.11.11 Shopping for elderly or handicapped 1.11.12 Recycling plastic bags 1.11.13 Education leaflets 1.11.14 Special offers, e.g. free gifts 1.11.15 Free bones for dog 1.11.16 Storage of customer's frozen goods, if required 1.11.17 Itemized receipt		

Section 2   The service delivery characteristics (which may not be seen by customer)

2.1   The supplier/delivery process

2.2   Security

2.3   The microbiological/refrigeration process

2.4   The storage period/system

2.5   Maintenance

2.6   Safety of sub-contractors (which can be managed under the Health and Safety system)

2.7   Environmental probity/awareness of suppliers (which can be managed under 2.1 above or an environmental management system using ISO 14000 as a guide or the controlling mechanism)

2.8   An ISO 9000 quality management system (which may cover all of the quality issues here and in Section 1 above, as a guide or the controlling mechanism for service quality).

Manufacturers

This section is mainly the concern of the sales and administration departments of manufacturing companies. It is *not* aimed at manufacturing facilities. Manufacturers who have not already implemented either ISO 9000 or ISO 14000 systems should not use the service-oriented approach shown here as they will need separate, but linked, management systems for quality, environmental management and health and safety. They should consult other books such as *ISO 14000 and ISO 9000* (Rothery, 1995).

The sales and administration departments of manufacturing companies are services companies, and should implement most if not all of the systems shown here, using the full track approach shown in Chapter 3.

They should simply rewrite the text of their manufacturing facility's Quality Manual, so that it reads as services rather than manufacturing, remove the design paragraphs, if any, unless they are designing services (in other words use ISO 9002 rather than ISO 9001), design appropriate control documents, and use two other parts of this book for the all-important procedures. These two parts are the system shown for retail stores, shortly, and their own version of the Quality Procedures Manual for dealerships shown in Appendix I. This is the most generically suitable set of procedures for manufacturers.

Service stations

For help and advice with this section, this author is indebted to Texaco. This section is written in the form of full procedures as distinct from the checklist approach used in the previous sections for hotels and supermarkets, and, thus, could serve as a model for the kind of full procedures needed within each service industry.

Forecourt Procedures for Service Stations

1 Servicing and care of equipment

1.1 Pumps must be maintained in proper condition. The hoses and nozzles should be in good order at all times. Each pump should have the grade of fuel clearly described. Pumps must have an electrical certification to DSA (Dangerous Substances Authority) standards and this certificate must be available for inspection.

1.2 Pumps must be calibrated by the Weights and Measures Inspector, sealed and a certificate of calibration obtained. This certificate should specify traceability to a recognized National Standard and must be retained for inspection. Additional or replacement or repaired pumps must be calibrated and sealed before being put into service. Where a seal is broken, the Weights and Measures Inspector must be informed and a record retained.

1.3 Air lines and gauges should be maintained in good condition. Gauges should be calibrated annually with traceability to a recognized National Standard and should be checked on an ongoing basis.

1.4 Air compressors should be maintained in working condition. A current Insurance Engineer's Inspection Certificate must be available for inspection.

1.5 All equipment provided for customer use in the service area should be clean and in good condition. Broken or damaged equipment should be removed immediately.

1.6 Where car wash machinery is provided, it should be serviced and maintained strictly in accordance with the manufacturer's recommendations. Where any doubt exists as to the serviceability of a machine, it should be withdrawn from service and repaired, particularly if there is risk of damage to a customer's vehicle.

1.7 Where lifts and/or hoists are provided, the current inspection certificates should be available. They should be checked regularly to ensure they are in good condition.

1.8 In cases where thermometers are used for checking refrigeration and cool cabinets, a current Certificate of Calibration (traceable to a recognized National Standard) must be available. These calibrations must be carried out annually. The date of the next calibration should be clearly marked on the instrument. These instruments should be stored in a safe area to avoid damage.

1.9 Where 'insecticutor' units are in use, the replacement date of the neon light must be clearly shown on the unit.

2 Forecourt product handling

2.1 Product handling at the forecourt and ancillary storage facilities must be carried out in accordance with the Dangerous Substances (Retail and Petroleum Stores) Regulations, S/1/79/311, and a copy of these regulations must be kept on site. In addition, a Licence to Sell Hydrocarbons must be available on site. Operators should have a DSA Licence to operate.

2.2 Particular care must be taken during offloading of volatile fuels to ensure that there are no naked flames, lights, or other ignition sources in the vicinity.

2.3 All exits to the site should be kept clear during offloading of motor fuels.

2.4 A Schedule 4 Form must be completed prior to and during offloading of motor fuels in accordance with statutory regulations.

2.5 Truck dips should be checked and recorded before and after deliveries by an appointed person and the delivery docket signed.

2.6 Staff should be fully conversant with the procedures governing handling of product at the forecourt and this should be recorded in the training plan and the employee's record.

3 Dry goods inward

3.1 Proper storage facilities should be provided for all dry goods. Oil-based products should be stored in a separate store to dry goods for retail sale in the shop.

3.2 Deliveries should be checked against delivery documentation by a designated person and signed off accordingly.

3.3 Goods should be stored on shelves only. A 'First In – First Out' policy should be in operation to ensure correct stock rotation. Stores should always be kept neat and tidy.

3.4 Where goods are rejected on receipt, or removed from stock for return to a supplier, a segregated area or container should be provided, clearly marked to prevent inadvertent sale of the product.

4 Staff hygiene and dress

4.1 Staff must be trained in proper hygiene procedures and a record of this training must be made on the training record and on the employee's record.

4.2 Hands should be washed frequently throughout the day. In particular, persons who have various duties should always wash their hands before serving food.

4.3 Where unwrapped or loose food is served, it is essential that staff are fully trained in the hygiene procedures and wear appropriate clothing, i.e. hat, apron and disposable gloves.

4.4 Uniforms and protective clothing must be issued to each member of staff as appropriate to their duties. The standard uniform must be worn at all times when on duty.

4.5 Staff should be encouraged to present themselves in a neat and tidy appearance at all times while on duty.

5 Wine and liquor sales

5.1 In cases where wines and liquor are sold, the appropriate licence should be in place and displayed. Staff should be aware of the law regarding the sale of liquor to ensure compliance.

6 Hygiene and housekeeping – internal areas and shop

6.1 A documented procedure should be in place to ensure that daily checks are carried out and recorded. This should be in the form of a checklist with space provided for recording the results of the inspection of each separate area. In particular the following areas should be addressed:

- floors should be cleaned on a daily basis, or more frequently if required
- windows, doors, shelving, display units and counters should be cleaned as required and maintained in a neat and tidy condition
- stock, and goods for resale should be regularly checked to ensure that the merchandise is in proper condition for sale, is attractively displayed and is within the sell by date. Each item of merchandise for resale should be priced
- fridges and cool cabinets should not be filled above the load line
- a temperature record chart should be maintained to record daily temperature checks. These checks should be documented as to frequency and area to be checked, e.g. shop, store, display cabinets, coolers, fridges, freezers, and so on. As a guideline, display units should be maintained within the following limits:

Frozen foods cabinets	$-18°C$ to $-20°C$
Ice cream cabinets	$-23°C$
Dairy products cabinets	$+2°C$ to $+8°C$
Service over units	$0°C$ to $+3°C$

- a pest control procedure should be in place and records maintained. Insect control equipment should be checked and cleaned on a regular basis
- shop lighting should be checked to ensure it is in working order and failed bulbs and tubes promptly replaced.

7 Hygiene and housekeeping – toilets

7.1 An inspection and cleaning schedule should be in place to ensure that floors, toilet bowls, wash basins, dispensing and disposal facilities, towel cabinets, sanitary cabinets and air freshener units are cleaned daily, or more frequently as required. This should be in the form of a checklist with space provided for recording the results of the inspection of each separate area. In particular 7.2 and 7.3 should be addressed.

7.2 Consumables, (toilet rolls, soaps, towels, wipes, air fresheners, and so on) should be checked regularly and replaced as required.

7.3 Lighting should be checked to ensure it is in working order.

8 General housekeeping – external areas

8.1 A formal daily inspection procedure should be in place to ensure continuous good housekeeping and tidiness. This should be in the form of a checklist with spaces provided for recording the results of the inspection of each separate area. In particular the following areas should be addressed:

- the forecourt must be kept clean and tidy at all times. Suitable bins should be provided for litter. Bin liners should be used and the bins checked and emptied as required. Water should be always available in suitable containers. Windscreen washing facilities should be provided and replenished as required
- all external flood lighting, advertising lighting, and overhead canopy lighting should be checked to ensure it is functioning properly
- signs and lettering should be checked for cleanliness. Any damage should be repaired promptly
- product price lists should be clearly displayed in accordance with statutory requirements
- pumps and nozzles should be cleaned thoroughly on a daily basis, or more frequently if required
- a formal pest control procedure should be in place. Bait boxes should be provided and a record maintained of servicing and inspections
- where car wash facilities are provided, these should be kept clean and tidy and all cleaning materials and equipment properly stowed

- where service bays are provided, these should be kept clean and tidy. All tools and equipment should have suitable storage facilities
- boundary walls, fences and areas at the rear of buildings should be checked periodically for wind blown debris and kept tidy
- grass areas should be kept trimmed and neat and beds and borders attended to as required.

9 Safety and emergency procedures

9.1 A fire emergency plan must be displayed in a prominent position and all staff must be trained in the emergency procedures. This training must be recorded in the training record and in the employee's personal file.

9.2 Emergency phone numbers must be displayed adjacent to the main phone.

9.3 Fully serviced fire extinguishers should be placed at strategic points adjacent to the forecourt and buildings. Ensure that the correct type of extinguisher is provided at each area and ensure that a fire extinguisher colour code chart is displayed. Extinguishers should be marked boldly, easily accessible, and fully serviced at all times. The date of the last inspection and the due date of the next inspection should be written on a tag attached to each unit.

9.4 All entrances and exits should be kept free of obstruction.

9.5 Adequate safety signs should be provided to alert the public to hazards and to assist in implementing emergency procedures.

9.6 A safety statement in accordance with statutory regulations must be displayed in a prominent position.

10 Spillage of motor fuels and oils

10.1 Documented procedures must be in place for dealing with any spillage which may arise. These procedures should address the specific steps for dealing with each type of product on site. They should include: containment of the spillage, disposal, dispersal and clean-up options, evacuation of the site (if required), reporting procedures to head office and/or local authority.

10.2 Interceptors should be inspected at least four times per annum and the inspection recorded. They should be fully cleaned out annually by an authorized disposal contractor.

10.3 Suitable absorbent material, or sand buckets filled with dry sand, must be provided at pump islands.

10.4 All employees must be conversant with these procedures and the training recorded on the training record and in the employee's file.

11 Advertising and promotional material

11.1 It is company policy that all advertisements and promotions should be legal, decent and honest and should ensure that no offending material is used.

11.2 All outdoor display and promotional material should be kept neat and attractive.

12 Customer complaints

12.1 Customer complaints must be recorded on the customer complaint form. Where complaints are received by phone or mail, a 48-hour response system should be in place to ensure prompt attention.

12.2 The customer complaint form should be designed to accommodate the following:

- the name, address and telephone number of the complainant
- the nature and detail of the complaint and the date of receipt
- the name of the person who received the complaint
- the follow-up action proposed to resolve the complaint
- the person designated to implement the follow-up action
- The date of completion of the follow-up action.

12.3 Customer complaints should be retained for review at regular intervals and corrective action implemented where appropriate to prevent a recurrence.

12.4 The effectiveness of the corrective actions should be reviewed annually.

13 Data collection and recording

13.1 Sales of motor fuels must be recorded on a daily basis and reconciled with physical stocks. Reports showing variances against budget must be prepared.

13.2 An incident reporting procedure must be in place together with a record of the follow-up action taken.

13.3 Customer service quality surveys must be carried out periodically, and the results recorded and reviewed in pursuance of the quest for continuous quality improvement.

General dealerships

The code of practice concerning general dealerships is one of the more developed in this book and is presented as a full set of quality procedures in Appendix I.

To put this in perspective once again, one needs a Quality Manual, quality control documents and a set of quality procedures, which in a services company can also contain environmental and health and safety procedures.

The quality procedures shown in Appendix I would suit most dealerships, such as spare parts, but they could also be easily adapted to suit car and other equipment dealers.

Retail stores

An overview of a comprehensive system for retail stores follows. This can be used either for retail stores or as a model for all of the services sectors.

A sample retail store system

What follows is an outline of a comprehensive system for retail stores, aimed at both chain stores and stand alone stores. It incorporates quality, environmental management, health and safety, and also attempts to provide protection against charges of negligence and opportunistic claims for compensation in the general trading areas covered under quality, health and safety and environmental management.

For this to be of use to service sectors other than retailing, simply replace the code of practice shown under Section 7, which is the stores procedures, with the appropriate procedures for your services sector, or apply your own versions of one of the codes of practice shown in this part of the book.

The system is called Storepac and it is shown here in outline form only, for reasons of space. Studied carefully however one should note that much of what it requires is shown elsewhere in the book in summary form. It is probably the first such 'package' to be developed for a retail store or chain stores, and as such might serve as a model for service companies in general. It was developed by this author as a services follow-on to the *KEYPAC 2000* series of packages for manufacturers published by Gower. Should the reader be interested in knowing more about this approach and other 'benchmarks' being developed for the services sector, fuller information can be obtained by accessing the Internet site http://ireland.iol.ie/grandslam and http://ireland.iol.ie/rothery.

Storepac outline

1   Description
2   Issue identification
3   Quality/customer requirements
4   Environmental probity
5   Health and safety
6   The major documents
7   The store procedures

1 Description

This section is based on a new package called Storepac, designed by this author, with two purposes in mind. First, as a package to meet the quality, environmental and health and safety requirements of retail stores, including chain stores, and, second, as a generic model for the whole services sector. The experience for this was this author's existing KEYPAC product, which, while originally aimed at general manufacturers with an engineering bias, subsequently became the generic model for a range of manufacturing industries, including chemicals, print and packaging and food and drink.

Storepac is a package of generic documentation, which prompts users for the extra information needed for a specific store, for *managing the key issues* of quality, environmental probity, staff health and safety, public safety and product liability. The reason for this choice is that all of these issues are subject to either mandatory market requirements or compulsory legislation, or both.

Another reason for the choice is that these issues can also be managed under two standards, which are ISO 9000 and ISO 14000.

Here is a simple description of the package: *it is the generic docu-mentation for stores, especially chain stores, for the three key issues of quality, environmental management and staff health and safety, which are covered by standards and regulations.*

The outline of the contents of the package discussed here allows a good overview of the kinds of systems discussed in this book which are needed by a retail store or chain store.

The package is already customized as far as possible to the retail sector, with chain stores and single retail outlets in mind. The text shows where certain 'store specific' and 'local specific' information, such as local regulations, should be inserted, and makes suggestions concerning where the information can be obtained – from certain suppliers for example. Apart from such highly company-specific information, much of the balance is generic and common to all companies in the retail store sector.

2 Issue identification

Under an 'Issue identification' heading a questionnaire asks the store a series of questions concerning the following important issues:

- the service and product liability exposure in dealing with customers and one's knowledge of this situation
- where there are single large and sophisticated customers, the service brief or contractual arrangements
- the service brief advertised to all customers, and the consumer rights and advertising legal requirements
- the legal requirements of raw materials, components and services procured from suppliers (vendors)
- the legal requirements of the materials and components (or substances) handled by staff

- the legal requirements of the tasks engaged in by staff
- the health and safety regulations with specific information for the EU and the US
- the major environmental requirements – emissions, discharges, waste, noise, odour, public safety, and so on
- emergency response considerations.

3 Quality/customer requirements

This section contains the following:

- a list of required documents
- a generic or model Quality Manual for retail stores
- staff training material.

4 Environmental probity

The following are examples from this section:

- initial environmental review
- environmental management programme
- register of effects
- control and monitoring manual
- environmental management manual
- pre-certification checklists, audit material, other.

5 Health and safety

The main elements here are:

- awareness of the considerable risks for individual managers as well as for companies
- the health and safety manual
- list of SOPs – standard operating procedures
- local laws such as EU and US health and safety regulations
- staff training.

6 The major documents required

The key documents required for ISO 9000 are:

- document list
- quality Manual
- quality procedures manual
- training material
- pre-certification checklist
- a list of the actual generic quality procedures or 'codes of practice' for retail stores. See below.

The key documents required for ISO 14000 are:

- issue identification questionnaire
- outline Register of Regulations
- initial environmental review
- environmental management programme
- register of effects
- control and monitoring manual
- training course for staff
- pre-certification checklist
- generic or model health and safety manual
- list of health and safety standard operating procedures (SOPs).

7 The store procedures

(This is the code which this author converted into codes of practice for other services sectors, such as accountants and banks.)

   Below is an outline of the contents list of a code of practice for retail and chain stores.

1 Shop front (including where relevant reception/telephonist; order/enquiry procedures although managed under the QMS or ISO 9000 system will be detailed here also)
2 Capacity/accessibility
3 Personnel/including staff dress
4 Products/services
5 Waiting time/responsiveness
6 Hygiene/housekeeping (including toilets)

7 Safety and emergency procedures (managed under the health and safety system)
8 Courtesy
9 Comfort/aesthetics
10 State of the art technology
11 Effective communication
12 Range of services
13 Servicing equipment
14 Yard and storage handling procedures
15 Supplier (vendor) management
16 Special categories of product/service – food, wine and liquor, gasoline
17 Advertising and promotional material
18 Customer complaints/returns and other feedback
19 Environmental management system using ISO 14000 as a guide or the controlling mechanism for all environmental issues, including transport where there are chain stores
20 Quality management system using ISO 9000 as a guide or the controlling mechanism
21 Product/service liability
22 Continually assessing the potential for charges of negligence or opportunistic claims for compensation from the public
23 Purchase of supplies and services from approved (approved in advance by you) suppliers only.

The reader who would like to try to use this template to develop full procedures for a store could also use the procedural manuals shown for both service stations and car dealers as a guide.

Solicitors and the legal profession

In 1993, the Legal Practice Directorate of The Law Society in the UK published a code of practice for solicitors entitled 'Practice Management Standards'. This appears to be suitable for lawyers also, particularly as they interface with the customer through solicitors.

The code takes the BS 5750 (ISO 9000) standard and interprets its 20 main quality system steps so that they relate to the procedures within a legal practice. It notes that the standard says what has to be done, but not *how* it should be done, which is a seldom seen explanation of why we need codes of practice by sector in the first instance.

Here is an outline of the elements needed in a code of practice for solicitors. These would be reflected in summary form in the Quality Manual, and would be the headings for detailed procedures in procedures manuals.

First the overall or Quality Manual level considerations.

- Adopt a policy of quality, preferably implemented through ISO 9000, construct an organization, assign responsibility and resources.
- Construct the necessary documentation and system.
- Create specifications for all dealings with clients, including brief requirements, terms, service to be supplied.
- Construct or formalize a methodology for selecting and briefing counsel, expert witnesses, and others.
- Construct or formalize a methodology for planning, dealing with and monitoring the progress of each case, including:
  responsibility for material supplied by the client
  case reference and monitoring
  internal inspection
  feedback on mistakes, complaints or faults
  remedial action
  safeguarding of documents
  checking of all information used.
- Construct or formalize a methodology for controlling handling of documents, including case files, precedents, and so on.
- Training – keeping up to date with developments in the law
  – in the quality system, client care, case management.
- Internal quality audits on a regular basis. Built in checks to ensure that the quality system is working at least once a year.
- Statistical or other relevant analyses of performance.

Moving to the detailed level of the procedures manual, the fundamental procedure on which the quality performance depends, or 'customer service', is that section known as case management. An outline code of practice for a case management system follows:

At a general level

Maintain documentation, numbering and indexing systems.
Establish a production control system to ensure that the capacity exists

for individual staff members to deal properly with the number of cases assigned to them. Perhaps the greatest quality weakness in the legal profession is for professionals not to have the time to deal with cases. This may be more true of barristers, and is probably caused by their taking on too many cases, resulting in quantity rather than quality, a very dangerous situation for them in this new era of increasing accountability. Already journalists and authors are noticing this, as are expert witnesses who may be in court. Judges also see it, not to mention unfortunate fee-paying clients. This may be the single most important part of the quality system for solicitors and barristers, to learn from manufacturing and to employ proper production, or work flow, techniques.

Indeed, the same computerized system which maintains the work programme of each professional can also maintain the next important schedule – that which monitors and signals key events, expiry of a limitation period, or time limits for reviews or applications, and so on.

The system can also specify and monitor the appropriate authorization levels or persons for prescribed activities or undertakings, as well as any third-party funding arrangements.

At the detailed level of client care or case management

An enquiry/order action system which ensures that all requests for service are dealt with properly.

Full procedures to ensure compliance with the established national or regional legal practice, including established cost schedules. The costs should be available in checklist or standard letter form for clients.

A written procedure for taking instruction from clients, recording advice given, action to be taken, terms of business, the likely cost, who will be involved from the company or counsel, and dates where known, all confirmed in writing to the client.

The monitoring system should be used to keep clients informed of progress and to monitor that this information is sent to clients and acknowledged.

The systems used by manufacturing to manage procurement or suppliers can also be used to manage the services bought in or secured from barristers or other experts.

There should be an approved list, specifying both expertise and previous performance, especially for counsel who should be subjected to the rigours of performance evaluation. This is the place to identify the lawyer who cannot find time to read the client file because of too much work. The selection criteria should include both recommendation and *availability*.

The above has been a sampling only, so please consult the Law Society's Practice Management Standards document for the construction of a full set of procedures.

Accountants

Accountancy is a most interesting area for this subject. First, it is the practice with the longest standing and virtually unchanged code of main practice, the procedure for doing accounts. It is also the only other general management code after environmental management, health and safety and quality in the product liability and customer rights sense to be backed by the law. You can have bad planning and marketing and product development and production, even if it puts you out of business, but it is illegal to have bad or inadequate accounting, health and safety or environmental management.

While its main procedures of profit and loss and balance sheet may be long-established, accountancy, like all other services badly needs service standards if its practitioners are to survive. They have lost out on much else – the computer revolution, quality and environmental management and auditing, so it will be very serious for them if they are also slow to adopt services standards.

Codes of service quality are hard to come by in the accounting profession. Using the code of practice for retail stores as the base, the author drew up a services code for accountants as follows:

- the shop front, the reception/telephonist, and quality and efficiency of response
- order/enquiry procedures backing up the shop front
- capacity/accessibility. A documentation and indexing and production control system along the lines of those discussed for solicitors above
- personnel/including staff dress
- products/services (a correct or relevant and comprehensive range of services)
- waiting time/responsiveness managed under the production control system
- hygiene/housekeeping (including toilets; clients of accountants also use toilets)

- safety and emergency procedures (managed under the health and safety system)
- courtesy (managed under shop front and personnel above)
- comfort/aesthetics
- state of the art technology
- effective communication
- servicing equipment (relevant to office and IT equipment)
- yard and storage handling procedures (not relevant except perhaps for client car parking)
- supplier (vendor) management. Probably not relevant
- special categories of product/service – consultancy, for example, or legal work
- advertising and promotional material
- customer complaints and other feedback
- environmental management system using ISO 14000 as a guide or the controlling mechanism for all environmental issues, including transport (staff cars)
- quality management system using ISO 9000 as a guide or the controlling mechanism
- product/service liability
- continually assessing the potential for charges of negligence or opportunistic claims for compensation from the public.

The surprise in the above was in how similar a code of good service practice is for both accountants and retail stores.

At the detailed or client procedures level one needs procedures for:

- initial interview enquiry records
- letter of engagement
- index to and control of working papers
- standard audit packs for private individuals, private and public companies
- standard letters to banks, solicitors, company registration offices, usually laid down by the accountancy associations
- forms of authorization for obtaining information from third parties
- generic accounting report formats, sample audit report
- generic audit report formats.

Banks

Banking may be one of the first service sectors to have ISO codes of practices, or what ISO is calling 'product standards' for its services. A bank should have a very special interest in quality and environmental/ health and safety codes of practice, first as a large service company dealing daily with thousands of customers it has a large services brief, and second, almost uniquely, except perhaps for insurance companies, it has a big vested interest in the continuing welfare of its customers after they leave the premises. Because of this, it is a wonder that banks have not been more to the front in producing codes of good business and services practice both for themselves and their customers.

Once again we take the basic retail store code of practice, shown above, and convert it to a code of practice for a bank:

- the shop front, the reception/telephonist, and quality and efficiency of response
- order/enquiry procedures backing up the shop front
- capacity/accessibility. A documentation and indexing and production control system along the lines of those discussed for solicitors above
- personnel/including staff dress
- products/services (a correct or relevant and comprehensive range of services)
- waiting time/responsiveness managed under the production control system
- hygiene/housekeeping
- safety and emergency procedures (managed under the health and safety system)
- courtesy. Managed under shop front and personnel above
- comfort/aesthetics
- state of the art technology
- effective communication
- servicing equipment (relevant to office and IT equipment)
- yard and storage handling procedures (not relevant except perhaps for client car parking)
- supplier (vendor) management. Probably not relevant
- special categories of product/service – business advice, property purchase, mortgages, savings, investments, pensions, for example, or legal work

- advertising and promotional material
- customer complaints and other feedback
- environmental management system using ISO 14000 as a guide or the controlling mechanism for all environmental issues, including transport (staff cars)
- quality management system using ISO 9000 as a guide or the controlling mechanism
- product/service liability
- continually assessing the potential for charges of negligence or opportunistic claims for compensation from the public.

Once again it is striking how similar a code of good service practice is for both banks and retail stores.

At the detailed or customer procedures level one needs procedures for:

- initial interview/enquiry records
- letter of agreement/engagement
- index to and control of files and working papers
- standard procedures for assessing customers worth, risk or potential for private individuals, private and public companies
- standard letters to solicitors, company registration offices, other
- forms of authorization for obtaining information from third parties
- generic accounting report formats. Sample audit reports
- generic audit report formats.

Restaurants

While this book uses the retail store as the model for all services businesses, restaurants could as easily serve as that model; indeed, early drafts of the ISO 9004 Part 2 standard for services companies suggest that the authors were very influenced by restaurants in their first speculations about the feasibility of producing services standards.

Restaurants have a number of elements common to most services, chief amongst them the up-front activities seen by the customer, and, in the background, the kitchen and stores and supplier and grower which are not seen. They can also display a wide range of quality levels from gourmet food and friendly and efficient delivery to food poisoning and the soup dropped in one's lap. Interestingly, they could conceivably serve what appears to be, and tastes like, gourmet food and still give the customer a microbiologically generated bad stomach.

This writer was very surprised to find that awards such as Michelin did not look beyond the food served at the process and delivery, at least according to the one award-winning restaurant questioned. This author was not able to make contact with the London public relations office of Michelin to confirm or deny this, but if this is indeed the case such award-winning restaurants would not meet the requirements of ISO 9000 or ISO 14000.

Here is a proposed code of practice for restaurants, once again based on the retail stores model.

The 'Issue identification' stage

Are you, as the owner or manager, dealing with the following important issues?

- the service and product liability exposure in dealing with customers and your knowledge of this situation
- the menu clearly laid out with full descriptions and prices
- meals delivered strictly to the menu
- the correctness and quality of raw materials and services procured from your suppliers
- the legal requirements of the materials and components (or substances) handled by staff
- the legal requirements of the tasks engaged in by staff
- the health and safety regulations
- the important environmental requirements – emissions, discharges, waste, noise, odour, public safety, and so on
- emergency response considerations.

The restaurant procedures

Full procedures should be in place, preferably written into manuals, for the following issues:

1 Maintaining the condition of the shop front, and the quality of service at reception, including the telephonist, and a table booking or reservation system.

2 Maintaining reasonable and legal capacity and accessibility.

3 Personnel/including staff dress.

4 Maintaining, and improving where possible, the range of meals and menus.

5 Waiting time/responsiveness targets and a monitoring system.

6 Hygiene/housekeeping procedures (including toilets), apart from kitchen.

7 Safety and emergency procedures (managed under the health and safety system).

8 Courtesy.

9 Comfort/aesthetics (including meeting the legal and comfort requirements of non-smokers), and relevance or 'quality' of background music played, in most cases not commercial radio or television, unless nature of the 'diner' or 'pub' demands them.

10 State of the art technology, including correct and prompt billing and acceptance of payment.

11 Effective communication.

12 Detailed food preparation and kitchen procedures, including waiter and waitress routines, and microbiological requirements, over and above normal hygiene shown above, and full supplier procedures.

13 Servicing equipment.

14 Yard and storage handling procedures.

15 Supplier (vendor) management.

16 Special categories of product/service – liquor, wines.

17 Advertising and promotional material, over and above menus.

18 Customer complaints/returns and other feedback.

19 Environmentally managed disposal of waste and containers.

20 Quality management system using ISO 9000 as a guide or the controlling mechanism.

21 Awareness of legal responsibilities and exposure. Continually assessing the potential for charges of negligence or opportunistic claims for compensation from the public or staff, paying special attention to the regulations for
 – safe workplace
 – equipment
 – personal protective equipment
 – pregnant or breastfeeding workers
 – safety signs
 – all food and restaurant regulations
 – all hygiene regulations
 – emissions, noise, odours, or waste water discharges

– manual handling, such as the lifting of packages or cartons or pallets.
22 Purchase of supplies from approved suppliers only.

Other codes of practice

Here are some BSI codes of practice published under the title of *BSI Quality Assurance Publications*.

Most of these are guidance notes for the application of the ISO 9000 series to the named sector, while all can be used as the code of practice for the sector.

- Food and drink industry QGN/41/42/390: 1991
- QA System for Registered Stockists QSP/61/92002: 1992
- Hotel and catering industry QGN/66/392: 1992
- Banking and finance industry QGN/82/393: 1992
- Garages offering service, repair and sale of new unused vehicles QGN/6510/391: 1991
- Bodyshops offering a service of body repairs and repainting QGN/6710/387: 1991
- Transportation, storage and distribution industries QGN/7230/385: 1992
- Ship operations and ship management industries QGN/7400/389: 1991
- Education and training QGN/9310/395: 1992
- Management systems of schools QGN/9320/401: 1993
- Continuing nursing care sector QGN/9510/398: 1993
- The ambulance service QGN/9520/394: 1992
- Code of practice for the manufacture of pharmaceutical raw materials P00020: 1990
- Code of practice for the manufacture of printed materials for use in the packaging and labelling of medicinal products P00021: 1990
- Code of practice for the manufacture of medicinal product contract packaging materials P00022: 1990.

PART III

The Environmental Management Documentation

Introduction

The figure below shows the main documentation needed for the implementation and management of an environmental management system operating to the requirements of ISO 14000.

The main documentation needed to implement a comprehensive environmental management standard to the requirements of ISO 14000 is as follows.

- A report on the initial environmental review. This is a once-only document.
- Register of Regulations. This can be a ring binder describing the statutory instruments relating to the company's environmental activities, air, water, waste, noise, odour, and so on. It can also contain copies of the actual statutory instruments, should the company wish. Some further explanation of this register is given below.

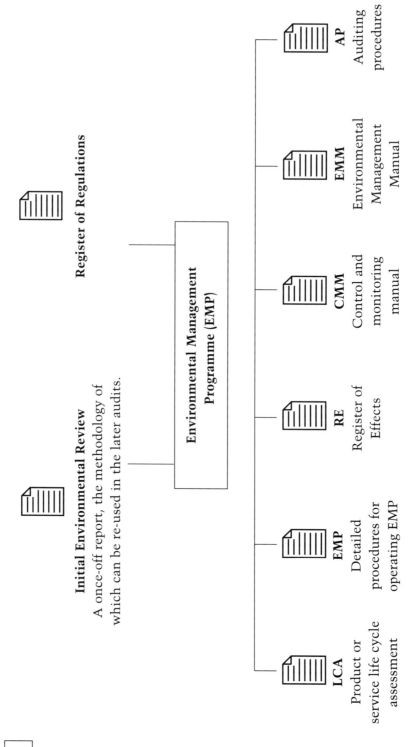

Register of Regulations

Initial Environmental Review
A once-off report, the methodology of
which can be re-used in the later audits.

**Environmental Management
Programme (EMP)**

LCA
Product or
service life cycle
assessment

EMP
Detailed
procedures for
operating EMP

RE
Register of
Effects

CMM
Control and
monitoring
manual

EMM
Environmental
Management
Manual

AP
Auditing
procedures

126

- A description of the procedures needed to operate the overall environmental management programme, including a method for analysing the issues involved or a full life cycle assessment procedure, also below.
- Register of effects. A register detailing the effects of activities on the environment, and the control of licensed or policy limits.
- Control and monitoring manual. This can be a ring binder containing the actual control documents, licences, and other official documents.
- Product life cycle assessment documentation, showing how the company has assessed its product or service activities from 'cradle to grave' – for example going back to the farm and out to the point where the customer may dispose of the container to assess all steps in the life cycle of a product or service.
- Auditing procedures and reports.
- Training records. These can also be in the control and monitoring manual.
- The Environmental Management Manual. This is the 'quality manual' of the environmental management system, and an outline of its contents is given below.

It is extremely unlikely that any service company could construct an environmental management system and its required documentation from the information given in this chapter, although the outline of the Environmental Management Manual below gives a good indication of the system needed. The reader intending to implement a full environmental management system should consult the books on BS 7750 and ISO 14 000 for fuller information on how this is done (Rothery, 1993; Rothery 1995).

In this context, the reader can be reminded that this book is attempting to provide service companies, small and large, with a basic system which ensures the maintenance of quality to the ISO 9000 standard, and the identification and meeting of all legal requirements in the areas of customer dealings, environmental probity and health and safety.

The most basic documentation needed, therefore, over and above a Quality Manual and health and safety records, are a Register of Regulations and a control and monitoring manual to ensure that the law is being met. One must constantly remember that even if one does not implement formal certifiable ISO 9000 and ISO 14 000 management systems the law must still be met, and, for convenience, the law can also be taken to include keeping customers satisfied.

Sample Environmental Management Manual

Doc No: EM–001	Company Inc.					Date of Issue: 01/01/97
	Environmental Management Manual					
Approved by:						Page No 5 of 27

0.2 Table of contents

Section	Clause*	Subject	No. of sheets
0.1		Document index	
0.2		Table of contents	
0.3		Amendment procedure	
0.4		Description of company	
1.0	4.1	Environmental management system	
2.0	4.2	Environmental policy	
3.0	4.3	Organization and personnel	
4.0	4.4	Environmental effects	
5.0	4.5	Objectives and targets	
6.0	4.6	Management programme	
7.0	4.7	Documentation	
8.0	4.8	Operational control	
9.0	4.9	Management records	
10.0	4.10	Management audits	
11.0	4.11	Management review	
12.0		Suppliers	

Annex 1   Letter to suppliers
Annex 2   Environmental management programme
Annex 3   Preliminary environmental review
Annex 4   Links with ISO 9000

* Clause relates to the number of the actual clause detailing this requirement in the ISO standard.

The Register of Regulations

The Register of Regulations can be in any form but should demonstrate that the company knows the law as it relates to its activities. A list of sample issues covered by legislation, codes of practice and policies for a company in a typical EU member state follows:

- physical planning
- EU EMAS regulation
- environmental impact assessment (over a certain size of operation)
- waste
- toxic waste
- raw materials
- transport
- packaging
- nuisance and noise
- handling of dangerous substances
- shipping of dangerous substances
- trees, amenities, landscape, and wildlife
- effluent discharges
- emissions
- use of materials
- use of energy
- product/service quality (that one delivers what is promised)
- public safety
- staff health and safety
- raw materials (that is the legislation relating to them)
- supplier/including services activities, such as transport.

(Note that some of these can also be codes of practice, and policies.)

Sample Register of Regulations page

Doc No: ERR–001		Company Inc.		Date of Issue: 01/11/96
		Register of Regulations		
Approved by:						Page No 7 of 43

Waste

Regulations

There are four regulations applicable to our operations. These are:
  European Communities (Waste) Regulations, 1979 (S.I. No. 390 of 1979);
  European Communities (Waste) Regulations, 1984 (S.I. No. 108 of 1984);
  The 4th and Final EC Directive on Packaging Waste;
  Litter Act No. 11 of 1982.

Policy

There are also principles and policies laid out in the EC document 'A Community Strategy for Waste Management SEC (89) 934 1989'. It is our policy to support the principles stated here in our operations.

The first of the above regulations demands that local authorities be responsible for the provision of waste management in our area. It is our policy to commit all of our normal waste to the local authority, or to a registered operator, registered under the 1978 regulations. It is our policy to check that all waste disposal operators used by us produce evidence of such registration. For as long as the local authority, or registered operator, continues to manage our waste this policy will apply. In the event of the local authority, or registered operator, not being able to manage our waste, we shall store it safely on site until the local authority resumes management, or until safe and legal alternative management can be arranged.

We will also ensure that our waste is recycled as far as possible.

Sectoral Codes of Practice for ISO 14000

The sectors covered are:

- print and packaging
- transport
- shipping
- waste management
- retail.

Print and packaging

When ISO 9000 began to sweep through manufacturing industry, first to adopt it were the large manufacturers. These quickly passed it on to their main suppliers such as raw materials and components vendors. Amongst the most rapid of these to respond were print and packaging suppliers, the reason being that traditionally they saw themselves as a part of the finished product of their customers.

This has begun to repeat with ISO 14000, the environmental management standard, and its forerunner, BS 7750, the British Standards Institution model upon which ISO 14000 was based.

What are now shown here in this section are the environmental management issues for print and packaging as distinct from the quality issues which will differ little from other manufacturing companies. Print and packaging is treated here as a service, although it is more of a manufacturing activity, the reason for this being that it shares with many other sophisticated suppliers the need to meet the requirements of a small number of large and highly sophisticated manufacturers, thus having to apply the most rigid codes of good service practice.

Fortunately there is already a BSI code of practice, called an 'application guide' for print and packaging companies, entitled 'BS 7750 Sector Application Guide for Printing and Packaging'. Since this emerged, a number of print and packaging companies have adopted BS 7750/ISO 14000 systems and it is their experiences which are used here.

The possible environmental issues which will have to have procedures written for their management and control in print and packaging companies are as follows:

- planning
- emissions to atmosphere
- effluent discharges
- water-based waste
  - to storm drains
  - to foul drains
  - including discharge to drains from photographic area
  - including discharge from plate/screen preparation
  - purification or stabilization of discharges
  - avoidance of leakage to surface drains
  - reclamation of water from screen or plate making area
  - drains complying with regulations for separation of storm and foul water
  - solvent recovery system
  - ink UV or water based
- disposal/treatment of spent solvents

- disposal/treatment of waste ink
- disposal/treatment of waste varnish
- disposal/recycling of off-cut materials
- disposal/recycling of solvent containers
- disposal/recycling of waste ink and varnish containers
- managing waste from
  - paper
  - board
  - card
  - adhesives
  - liners
  - metal
  - plastics
- in-house materials usage managed under a materials minimization programme
- energy conservation programme
- noise
  - in-house
  - fenceline
- smells
  - fenceline
- handling of dangerous substances, including staff procedures, separation in storage and use and emergency procedures for spillages, containment, and fire
- raw materials management
  - paper and board from managed forests
  - environmental probity of paper and board mills
  - environmental probity of ink and other component suppliers
  - chlorine free materials
  - other chemical-free raw materials considerations
  - packaging of raw materials
  - recycling possibilities
  - better choice of raw material for reduction in waste, in better sizes or containers, bigger units, drums rather than tins, avoidance of oil extraction or mineral mining
- alternative surface finishing processes which do not use solvents
- intermediate materials which are subsequently thrown away, such as protective sheets on surface, scrap paper used for note pads, received packing paper used for despatch, interleave paper used for packing or make ready

- enough ink only for the job mixed
- inks re-used by re-colour matching.

Transport

Here as in print and packaging we are fortunate to have a code of practice for environmental management. Published by the UK Road Haulage Association, it is entitled 'BS 7750 Sector Application Guide for Transport and Distribution Services'. The information used here, while compared for completeness against that document, is based on this author's experiences with transport companies.

This author was also fortunate, during the writing of a book about outsourcing, to have obtained a copy of the agreement between The Body Shop and the Lane Group which is used to maximize environmental management in the transport of product to the many Body Shop stores, and which was very useful to both the writing of the outsourcing book and this book.

This agreement entails lessons both in quality and environmental management as the Body Shop, the principal, saw their transport supplier, the Lane Group, as not just representing them in the Body Shop supply chain, but as a part of them – thus the wearing of Body Shop uniforms by Lane Group drivers. The Lane Group's primary responsibility was to ensure the safe and timely delivery of product from the distribution warehouse into the high street shops, in doing so being at the front line with the shops, and ensuring that the efforts made by the other elements of the supply chain were not wasted by a poor level of service at the final delivery.

The contractual arrangement between the two partners was formalized in a document called 'The Partnership Document', which reflects the day-to-day operation of the contract, details the management resources, the performance standards, the method of performance review and the broad financial arrangements, and includes important information on environmental considerations which help us in establishing a code of practice for all transport companies.

One of the main sections of the document was entitled 'Environmental targets', and it included the identification of the following environmental management issues:

- reduction in paper waste from delivery and other documentation
- reduction in fuel consumption – speed limits, re-routing schedules
- tyre usage – system of monitoring usage and set targets for reduction
- maximization of the use of resources from renewable services – including supplier management
- waste management
- evaluation of the reconditioning of parts instead of replacement
- environmental audits.

Moving from the Lane Group to transport companies in general, the following is an attempt at a list of the environmental issues needing management:

- planning/housekeeping
  - landscaping, affects on amenities, wild life, community
  - state of premises, hygiene, smells, noise
- operations
  - state of fleet
  - fuel management, consumption – speed limits, re-routing schedules
  - tyre usage management
  - fleet moving or standing discharges or emissions, such as oil and fuel spillage, odour, spill of substance being transported
  - moving or standing discharges to water, such as fuel and oil spillage, cleaning effluent
  - waste management of oils, replaced parts, tyres, cleaning fluids, rags, paper, cardboard, rubble
  - procedures for incidents, accidents, emergencies including contamination of soil through vehicle or container spillage or leaking storage
- general environmental and community issues, such as noise, dust, smells, smoke, unsightly yards, impact on landscape and the neighbourhood
- supplier management
- monitoring of industry developments
- monitoring of environmental standards and regulations
- an implemented environmental management system with full performance targets and audit procedures.

135

The BSI guidance notes for the transportation, storage and distribution industries

This document is titled *Guidance notes on the application of BS 5750: Part 2 to the transportation, storage and distribution industries*. For BS 5750 read ISO 9000.

Rather than repeating what is common to the other sectors in the code, the transportation, storage and distribution industries emphases only will be noted.

Contract review

The BSI notes put great emphasis on this, calling it 'paramount' to the quality management system. Unlike many other over the counter activities, they see every order accepted as a contract, not just a simple sale, requiring full recording of all communications including verbal, and the use of a formal contract.

The notes ask that both the extent to which individual staff can review contracts and the general conditions of each contract be laid down, and that there be a procedure to ensure that the purchaser's requirements are clear, that all differences are resolved, and that the terms of the order can be met.

The code requires an assessment of sub-contractors, as these may be fundamental to the service, covering elements such as vehicles, vehicle maintenance, tank cleaning, sub-contract drivers, training, maintenance, livery and so on. Sub-contractors should be selected on the basis of their ability to meet requirements, using 'documentary evidence' of a number of criteria including consistency of performance and reliability.

Process control is seen as the core of the operation and could include such specific activities as:

- cleaning of barrels/tankers
- handling/carriage of hazardous substances
- inspection/testing of hoses
- instructions to drivers
- loading/unloading
- maintenance procedures
- painting
- storage procedures

- vehicle modification
- welding.

Others common to many sectors but fundamental to transport are:

- calibration procedures for inspection and measuring equipment
- inspection and testing
- emergency procedures.

Also needed are handling and storage procedures.

Shipping

Environmental management standards is a very important subject for all shipping companies, as the International Maritime Organization, IMO, based in London, has produced a new code of practice, which is mandatory for all ships over a certain size by 1998 and mandatory for all by 2001.

The code of practice is called the ISM Code, and it is available from the International Maritime Organization at 4 Albert Embankment, London SE1 7SR.

In 1993 the IMO adopted a series of resolutions dealing with guidelines on management procedures to ensure the safest possible operation of ships and to reach a situation where there would be as little marine pollution as is reasonably possible. These adoptions of the resolutions resulted in the International Safety Management Code, known as the 'ISM Code'.

The ISM Code

The ISM Code is an international standard for the safe management and operation of ships and for pollution prevention.

At the instigation of the IMO, all governments of the world were asked to enact the necessary legislation to ensure that ships using their ports operated to the code. This is very similar to airlines who would not be allowed to fly into national airports without meeting the requirements of international aviation standards. Governments are concerned with both ship safety and the protection of their surrounding waters from pollution.

Realizing that neither ships nor shipping companies are similar or fully standardized, and that ships operate under a wide range of different conditions, the code was quite generic, but laying down certain general principles and objectives. In this respect it both followed the example of the ISO 9000 standard, and reflected its generic approach.

The resultant generality, while allowing a widespread application, demands customization at both the industry and the individual shipping company level. In its preamble the code states, 'Clearly, different levels of management, whether shore-based or at sea, will require varying levels of knowledge and awareness of the items outlined.'

The code is applicable to all ships. Some details of the ISM Code follow.

Care is taken to ensure that responsibility for the operation of any ship is assigned and clearly known to all authorities and interested parties. Responsibility is placed on the owner of the ship or any other organization or person such as the manager, or the bareboat charterer, who, according to the code, 'has assumed the responsibility for operation of the ship from the shipowner and who, on assuming such responsibility, has agreed to take over all duties and responsibility imposed by the Code'.

As its objectives, the code lists 'safety at sea, prevention of human injury or loss of life, and avoidance of damage to the environment, in particular to the marine environment and to property.'

The safety management objectives required by each company are almost a copy of any good code of safety practice, consisting of safe practices in ship operation, a safe working environment, the implementation of safeguards against the risks identified, and the ISO 9000 requirement of continuous improvement, in this case of safety-management as distinct from quality.

The requirements of the safety-management system read like a list of ISO 14000 requirements, but tend to state end objectives rather than practical procedures. For example, the demand for 'compliance with mandatory rules and regulations' and for 'the applicable codes, guidelines and standards' requires something very specific mentioned in ISO 14000 but not mentioned in the ISM Code. This is the important Register of Regulations, the device for assembling the regulations and codes in the first instance. One wonders if the writers of the ISM Code had access to either early drafts of ISO 14000 or the existing BSI 7750, which also lists the need for a Register of Regulations.

The system required is called a safety management system, or SMS, which is similar to the QMS, quality management system and EMS, environmental management system, concepts, but had it been based on either ISO 14 000 or the chemical industry's responsible care programme, one ISO 14 000-based EMS could have managed both safety and environmental considerations.

Almost mirroring both ISO 9000 and ISO 14 000, the SMS requires a safety and environmental protection policy and detailed procedures to ensure 'the safe operation of ships and protection of the environment in compliance with relevant international and flag-state legislation'. Also, as in the two ISO standards, it asks for 'defined levels of authority and lines of communication' and it wants these 'between, and amongst, shore and shipboard personnel'.

Two ISO 14 000 requirements are for procedures for reporting accidents and non-conformities with the code, and procedures to prepare for and respond to emergency situations.

Had ISO 14 000 been used as a model, its initial environmental review could have usefully been incorporated into the code as the initial appraisal, for, while the code asks for procedures for internal audits and management reviews, the importance of a major once-off or initial review at the time of adopting the standard seems to have been missed. Companies which have adopted ISO 14 000 and its earlier model, BS 7750, have found the initial environmental review, which can cover safety matters also, to be indispensable for identifying the significant issues needing control. If a company new to the system simply tries to practice audits, it may not know what to audit, or may miss vital legislation or key activities requiring audits.

Within the organization the ship's master is clearly named as the person on board equivalent to top management on shore, who, together with shore management, has the overall responsibility for implementing the safety and environmental protection policy of the company, and ensuring its management at ship level. He is of course also responsible for motivating and managing the crew in the carrying out of activities to the code, 'verifying that specified requirements are observed' and 'reviewing the SMS and reporting its deficiencies to the shore-based management'.

The company is responsible for the state of the ship and the qualifications and training and state of its master and crew.

Maintenance of the ship and its equipment is a vital SMS function as are emergency and navigation procedures. These involve the typical ISO 9000 procedures of inspections, reporting of non-conformities and their causes, corrective action and records.

A very important certification requirement is that a ship should be operated by a company which is issued a document of compliance relevant to that ship, which in turn means that it meets the requirements of the ISM Code. This is done through certification agencies named by each national government.

This document means that a company is deemed to be capable of complying with the requirements of the code by the agency and government of each relevant country. It must be carried on board so that the master, if asked, can produce it. In addition, a certificate, called a safety management certificate, will be issued to a ship, which verifies that the company and its shipboard management operate in accordance with the approved SMS.

The American Bureau of Shipping standard

The difference between the ISM Code and a standard published by the American Bureau of Shipping (ABS) is that the latter is much more comprehensive, allowing us to fill in many of the blanks left by the eight page ISM document. The 16 pages of the ABS document, however, still require detailed procedures before a ship can boast of having a full code of practice.

While it appears that the ISM Code is based on ISO 9000, the ABS standard is definitely based on it and on the ISM Code, being entitled 'Management Systems – Guideline for marine management and ship operation based on the requirements of ISO 9002 and the International Management Code for the Safe Operation of Ships and the Pollution Prevention (ISM Code)'.

It is an expansion of the ISM code to cover more operational issues, using as a guide the ISO 9000 standard. As one reads it, the pity that ISO 14000, or its earlier BS 7750, was not used becomes more apparent. ISO 9000 is about quality, not environment, health or safety. These two standards or codes, ISM and the American Bureau of Shipping standard, are about environmental, health and safety matters. Were they also covering such quality issues as satisfied customers in freight and passenger matters, those parts would be included as codes of practice in this book, but they are not, and one can only wonder why the more appropriate ISO 14000 standard was not used. The reason given by the American Bureau of Shipping is that many of the principles reflected in the management system requirements of the ISO 9000 series of standards are employed by the ISM Code, which appears to be saying that because the IMO used ISO 9000 we also are using it.

The ABS document goes on to say, 'The ISO 9000 series focuses management system elements on ensuring that customer requirements for quality are met. The ISM Code focuses a subset of the management system elements employed by the ISO 9000 series on ensuring the safe management and operation of ships and pollution prevention.' Here clearly it distinguishes between the two, as if saying we know we are not dealing with quality here but we can use the quality approach to deal with environment and safety, but they are saying this while ignoring the environmental and safety standard, and losing out doubly by not giving us a quality standard which would tell us how to treat our customers and passengers.

In a very revealing statement it adds, 'ISO 9002, however, does not provide marine industry specific guidance.' This can be taken as saying that because the IMO used the ISO 9000 quality management standard, we are using it, and because it does not include marine specific information we are now adding that information, which, while a very good explanation for the need for industry-specific codes of practice, still convinces one that they used the wrong standard. ISO 14000 has much more specific methodology on dealing with environmental and major incident and accident matters.

The ABS document gives the very specific explanation that the ISM Code is a management system code, or standard, 'designed with the objective of ensuring safety at sea, prevention of human injury or loss of life, and avoidance of damage to the environment, in particular, to the marine environment, and to property.' Their own guideline, on the other hand, 'is intended to be used as an aid to the interpretation of the requirements of ISO 9002 as applied to marine management and vessel operation'. At the same time, the ABS guideline also 'frames the requirements of the ISM Code within the context of the ISO 9002 elements'.

It then adds the sentence: 'A quality management system that complies with ISO 9002 should fulfil the requirements of the ISM Code.' This author thoroughly disagrees. A quality management system will deal with customer expectations and the fitness for purpose of the service or product. You can have a dirty, environmentally unsound and dangerous product if that is what the customer requires.

However the ABS standard does get down to the real procedures involved in shipping, without which we could not implement an ISM

141

code. Both ISO and the IMO have now produced generic management standards which are impossible to implement without detailed codes of practice which give them meaning at industry level. Each company or ship must take these to the next step of shop floor or 'deck' procedures.

The ABS standard brings us down to the levels of 'controlled conditions' which this author prefers to call 'issues requiring control'. These include ship and shoreside operations, compliance with classification requirements, maintenance of propulsion, navigation, and cargo handling equipment, properly maintained and calibrated equipment, procedures for the loading, transfer, discharge, and transportation of cargo, and the employment of trained and qualified personnel.

Deck operational procedures should cover: mooring, anchoring, port watches, pilot embarkation/disembarkation, fire and security watch, visitor control, stowaway search, and preparation for arrival/departure. It is fascinating to read such a list in a 'quality management' document and see neither customer nor passenger mentioned.

It is in this section, however, under the title of 'Process control' that we find the real hands-on shipping procedures under headings such as 'Deck operations', 'Cargo operations', 'Engine Room operations', 'Preventative maintenance', 'Navigation procedures', 'Safety procedures', 'Emergency preparedness', 'Ship's business', 'Technical procedures', 'Communication procedures', 'Ship Integrity procedures', and 'Pollution Prevention procedures'.

While these are very important guides to the areas which need procedures, they expand to mere headings only, such as, under 'Cargo operations', permit to work systems, helicopter operations, working aloft or over the side, heavy weather operations, and so on. It can be seen that detailed procedures are still required, but one must be thankful to the ABS for producing such a valuable template for the requirements.

The IMDG code

Like most other sectors with international activities, shipping is required to adopt codes other than its own. One of the most important of these is the IMDG code. This code is published and maintained by the International Maritime Agency (IMD), which is a UN agency. Its full title is the International Maritime Dangerous Goods (IMDG) Code. It is substantially harmonized with the ICAP, International Civil Aviation Organization Technical Instructions, and the IATA, Dangerous Goods Regulations.

Waste management

Another code of practice is available for waste management. Published by the Institute of Wastes Management, 9 Saxon Court, St Peter's Gardens, Northampton NN1 1SX, it is entitled 'Guidance notes for the applicability of BS 7750 to Waste Management'. Read ISO 14000 for BS 7750.

At the beginning of this document is the most interesting information that at least six regulatory bodies have produced seven sets of regulations with related documents to supervise waste management companies in their environmental activities. The documents include planning permission, procedures, licenses, emergency plans, consents, controls, while the regulatory bodies include planning authorities, fire authorities, local authorities, health and safety inspectorates, and water and river authorities.

At the end of the list is the amusing remark, 'This list is neither prescriptive nor exhaustive'.

So what could be added? Environmental protection agencies, consumer affairs agencies, revenue commissioners, labour tribunals, standards trading officers, the courts, and, finally, the customer.

As much of what would be relevant in a code of practice for waste management companies would be common to all transport and distribution companies, only a brief mention will be given here of the issues specific to waste management. The reader in that industry could use the transport code and ensure that these specific issues were included. Specific waste management procedures would include a priority section on emergency or 'abnormal operating conditions', in particular spillages, emissions, accidental chemical discharge, fire.

Central to the procedures will be a detailed section on the handling or treatment of waste by:

- landfill
- incineration
- chemical treatment.

Major issues involved and requiring detailed procedures and controls will be: emissions to atmosphere in the form of dust, fume, vapour or gas; contamination of land; discharges to water; accident and other spillages; solid and other waste management; affects on landscape and community; use of raw materials and energy; noise, smells, vermin and visual impact; management of dangerous or prescribed substances.

There may be at least four sites or 'operating theatres' involved, and these are:

- customer site
- transfer station
- vehicle on the roads
- treatment or disposal site.

All will require detailed procedures.

Retail

As most retail issues are quality or customer orientated, it has been convenient to include all of the environmental and health and safety requirements into the main set of procedures or code of practice. See, for example, the Storepac approach on page 107. Earlier we commented in some detail on what the likely retail environmental management issues will be. Here in broad summary form only are the environmental and staff and public safety issues common to most retailers:

- supplier management – ensuring the environmental probity of the supplied products and the environmental performance of suppliers and original manufacturers
- transport – using environmentally managed fleets, whether own or supplied
- staff health and safety
- customer safety, including emergency procedures
- planning, amenity, landscape, wildlife
- specialized retail and other services.

Most stores and chain stores will have the above issues, except that small chains and single stores will have little say in transport. Service stations will have critical safety and emergency considerations.

Hotels in common with supermarkets will have stringent micro-biological and hygiene considerations and together with super-markets and large chain or department stores stringent fire and emergency response procedures.

Banks will have a security element in staff and public safety, and fire and emergency procedures, while legal and other professions will have few environmental considerations other than staff transport, in-house materials and energy usage.

Staff and sub-contractors

Although strictly more health and safety than environmental, all services business should be aware of the legislated issues which arise in certain usually one-off or irregular working activities. Chapter 8 gives a list of activities from emergency and evacuation procedures to working in confined spaces which require written procedures and controls, and apply to both sub-contractors and staff.

Postscript: What Next?

One trend which has begun to dominate in industry, both manufacturing and services, and which looks set to increase for some years to come, is that of more precision and care in our activities. It is expressed mainly through management standards and controlled through regulation and certification.

It would not be an exaggeration to say that the concepts of truth and honesty are incorporated into the new regime, even legislated for and subjected to third-party verification. The new management standards are built upon such elements as exact specifications, precise procedures, processes and instructions, the minimization of waste, fitness for purpose, consistency of output, honest and correct descriptions, performance evaluation, the health and safety of workers and the community, and the protection of the environment.

Even the word 'quality', as used in the quality management standard, means something much more specific than up-market or aesthetic or valuable. It means consistency of product and process, exactness in specification, fitness for purpose, meeting the requirements.

So we have rigidly defined concepts, measurable elements, specifications for product, process and service, and independent certification schemes. All these now apply to manufacturing and to many service activities especially those, such as certain public utilities, which have critical safety implications. This public scrutiny or 'accountability' is now spreading into all of the main service categories – healthcare, hospitality, transport, banking, finance, insurance, transport, retail, and others.

There are two main drivers for this accountability – first demand from the public, second, the need to protect oneself against charges of negligence and opportunistic or justified claims for compensation.

It is inevitable therefore that this accountability will extend to the so-called 'social sciences', particularly to psychology in all its forms, including counselling and therapy, and even to the vaguest of the alternative sciences, the only test being whether there is a commercial activity involved, although in our new age of increasing regulation, even sports and leisure activities may not escape from accountability. The extension into the social industries will be as much driven by a need to cover oneself against claims for damages as by market demand, indeed even more when the backlash against the more disingenuous of these 'professions' takes place.

Had many of these stayed at the astrological level as alternative ways of life they might have remained outside the net of accountability, but they have been so much in the foreground giving 'expert witness' in litigatious disputes and even criminal actions, often giving opposite opinions for opposing counsel, that it is inevitable, and sooner rather than later, that they will have to demonstrate measurable standards and clear schemes of accountability.

These new systems of control, created to management standards, and accredited by certification schemes, will either reveal the fallacious and disingenuous nature of certain activities, or support their relevance. In turn, the certification schemes which will arise in support of the standards, will be backed up by legislation.

If anyone doubts this development, consider what a high state of accountability already exists in all spheres of industry, from manufacturing to air traffic control, from the High Street marketplace to the scientific laboratory. Exceptions in recent times were certain notorious state laboratories, which, lacking both quality standards and accountability, used contaminated results of tests as 'expert witness' against accused persons resulting in their imprisonment, one further example of the injustice which is certain to result from giving unlimited and uncontrolled powers to bureaucracies. Without systems of standards and measurement, and accountability, our modern technical world could not exist, nor could our forms of daily work and commerce. It will be seen that those parts of our lives involved with work and the commercial marketplace are highly standardized and regulated with visible systems of accountability in place from the weighing scales to the specification on the package. Backing up these standards in the commercial world are stringent legal regulations under such headings as product liability, public safety, consumer protection and misleading advertising. This creates a state of high accountability in our industrial and commercial activities, and makes dishonest dealings and cheating difficult.

In what we like to believe are the private spheres of home and community, there are also considerable levels of regulation and accountability. In the developed world one has little or no freedom to act outside of building regulations or to operate outside of the systems of water and energy and distribution, or telecommunications systems. On the streets, highways and waterways and in public places there are strict rules and regulations. One can ignore all of these but to do so incurs possible sanctions including penalties in the forms of fines or imprisonment.

Over millennia standard systems of weights and measures, together with detailed product and process specifications, have emerged which help to ensure fair trading and to protect citizens from exploitation, for even if a community is free from the more dramatic excesses of crime, trading is still regarded as a possible area for the emergence of human greed and avarice.

Many societies have believed that their very survival required law, independent of religion or morality. While some may see law as the hindering of individual freedom, many see it as the only means of securing individual freedom. Anyone whose life and limbs are threatened on the streets of cities and towns will support the latter view, considering that freedom has little meaning without protection from attack by others.

Now there are people who believe that to be robbed by a criminal is more honest than the deviousness and disingenuousness employed by those who masquerade as professionals in certain non-measurable so-called social sciences.

As the codes of practice and formal standards are developed for the vague services, those lacking them or lacking demonstrable systems of accountability become vulnerable to both criticism and the very kinds of legal action they have been supporting others in, in particular opportunistic claims for compensation.

As there are as yet no formal benchmarks to measure either their procedures or accountability systems against, let us put one together from what we know about emerging services standards and see how an operator in these businesses could fare.

We will assume that a therapist or counsellor has become the objective of an action for damages for negligence, or is named as a co-defendant in an action claiming defamation because of what is perceived by the plaintiff as false or reckless 'expert witness'.

We will now act as investigating inspectors and examine both the therapist/counsellor's management system and system of accountability, using the best benchmarks now available, the emerging codes of practice managed under quality management and environmental/safety management systems.

We begin with an issue identification procedure. Did the defendant know:

The laws as relating to all the activities, product/service liability, misleading advertising, consumer rights, defamation, libel, criminal negligence potential, in the case at issue?

The full customer requirements, and the full specifications for the service provided, according to industry accepted codes – in other words not the defendant's opinions as to assessing the customer's (patient's) needs, but an available industry set of routines?

The management system. If the above were known, what were the controls, the established limits, values, tests, evaluation procedures?

Where is the service brief advertised to all customers?

The above cover the top end of the management system (the ISO 9000 part); below this, should come the procedures, so the question can be asked, 'Where is the detailed procedures manual, for you and your staff if you have staff, showing the exact routines to be employed in each given situation?'

The defendant may reply, but my business is much too qualitative for such a system of accountability. The answers to that include the following: many services, such as restaurants, used to say that, only to find now that virtually everything they do is measurable; society will not continue to tolerate disingenuous operators who hide under labels of mysticism, which can come to be seen as charlatanism; at the end of the day the potential for damages for those lacking an open system of accountability may be so great as to make the practice of such a business far too risky.

High on the list of organizations likely to become the target for demands for accountability are 'victim support groups', who may in fact be political groups whose power and fund-raising are based on the existence of certain 'victims'. The benchmarks which will be applied here will be numbers actually fed and housed, not numbers 'counselled over the telephone', which cannot be verified or proven to be of any value.

Next will be benchmarks for the percentage of funds raised which charities spend on actual victims and the percentage spent on administration. Notorious recent cases of heads of charities, including senior religious persons, siphoning off funds for private use and living luxury private lifestyles have added an urgency to the need for benchmarks here. Independent third-party certification of how much is actually spent on real causes as advertised (in the services brief) will emerge.

What businesses will not come under such systems of public scrutiny and accountability? It is to be hoped that this will be all those which use creative talents, where of course the 'pseudo' and the gimmicky will still survive, and should in any free society. The world would be a poorer place were artists, musicians, poets and writers made to conform to codes of practice and systems of accountability, but this could be the subject of another book.

Quality Procedures Manual

Note

For reasons of space, only key parts of this manual have been included to give a flavour of the detail needed.

Doc No: EM–01	ServiceCo	Date of Issue: 01.01.98
	Procedures Manual	
Approved by:		Page No 1 of 15

ServiceCo

Quality Procedures Manual

Cover Page	
Page 1 of	Date: 01/01/97
Rev: 001	QA Mgr:
Doc No: EM–01	

This manual describes ServiceCo's quality procedures.

Alterations are not permitted without prior approval of the Quality Manager and must be applied used the system for amendment control contained within the Quality Manual.

0.1 Document index

Document number   *Title*

EM–1   Environmental Manual
QM–1   Quality Manual
ERR–1   Register of Regulations
ERE–1   Register of Effects
CMM–1   Control and Monitoring Manual

Doc No: EM–01	ServiceCo	Date of Issue: 01.01.98
	Procedures Manual	
Approved by:		Page No 2 of 15

S–1	Safety Statement
EP–1–11	Environmental Procedures
EP–11	Preventative maintenance system
QP–1	Non-Conforming Product
QP–2	Corrective Action
QP–22	Quality Records
QP–23	Training Procedure
QP–24	Customer Returns
QP–30	Internal Audits
QP–32	Final Inspection and Testing
QP–36	Management Review
TS–14	Environmental Training Syllabus
QD005	Approvals Sheet
BS 7750	Environmental Management System Standard
	Training course (use own reference number)

0.2 Document control procedure

Update this log when documents/procedures change. The quality manager is responsible for the maintenance of this log. Document master list can be found in the **Quality Manual** as the **Document index**.

Doc No: EM–01	ServiceCo	Date of Issue: 01.01.98
	Procedures Manual	
Approved by:		Page No 3 of 15

Quality Procedures Manual						
Proc No.	Change Revision No.	Date	Brief Description of Change	Section/s involved	Page Nos.	QM Signature

0.3 Document receipt form

This form is completed where changes are made in any documents and revised pages are issued to be inserted into the relevant manual.

Quality Procedures Manual				
Holders	Rev. No.	Date	Signature	Change Desc.

Doc No: EM–01	ServiceCo	Date of Issue: 01.01.98
	Procedures Manual	
Approved by:		Page No 4 of 15

This form must be signed by the relevant personnel when a revised page is issued to them by the quality manager. Old pages must be destroyed and revised editions inserted into the manual.

0.4 Document distribution list

Quality Procedures Manual				
Document	**Holder**	**Title**	**Receipt Date**	**Comments**

Description

This manual summarizes the procedures and practices for ServiceCo's operations at its NewTown facilities. The procedures are an integral part of ServiceCo's documented quality system and have been established in response to the requirements of ISO 9002.

Responsibilities and procedures have been established in the following areas:

Doc No: EM–01	ServiceCo	Date of Issue: 01.01.98
	Procedures Manual	
Approved by:		Page No 5 of 15

- reception
- accounts department
- sales department
- service department.

This is a controlled document as required by Section 3.3 of ServiceCo's quality manual.

Documentation management

The quality manager is responsible for managing this manual. He/she holds master copies of all controlled documentation and is responsible for amendments, and retrieval and disposal of obsolete sections as outlined in section 3.3 of the quality manual.

Changes to this document can only be made with the authorization of the quality manager, who is responsible for signing approval of amendments (see sections 0.2 to 0.4 of this manual).

Company description

ServicCo was set up in 1973 as a distributor of motor parts. We have the dealership for 12 leading manufacturers. We sell to a number of motor garages and shops throughout the country and also have our own shop on the premises. In addition, we have a service department which provides service and repair of parts.

1.0 Reception

1.1 General

Our reception area is usually staffed by one receptionist. However, during busy times another member of staff could be asked to help out in the

Doc No: EM–01	ServiceCo	Date of Issue: 01.01.98
	Procedures Manual	
Approved by:		Page No 6 of 15

reception area, where there are two functional PABXs. Also, when the receptionist is taking a break, another member of staff will usually take over in the reception area. In some cases, when there is nobody in the reception area, any member of staff can take responsibility for answering the telephone. We are aware that the reception area is the first point of contact with our customers and make it policy, therefore, to have the very highest standards in terms of courtesy and efficiency. These procedures should be followed when answering the telephone or greeting somebody in the reception area.

1.2 Telephone calls

The telephone should be answered promptly and clearly. The person answering the call should start off by saying 'ServiceCo, XXX speaking'. If the required individual is not available, the receptionist should ask the caller if they would like to speak to somebody else or if they would like to leave a message on the individual's voicemail. Because each staff member has a computerized diary, which is networked, the receptionist should be able to tell the caller if the individual is in a meeting, out of the office or away for an extended period. If the caller does not want to leave a message on the voicemail, they can leave a message with the receptionist who will mark it in her own computerized diary. While others answering a call can leave messages in this diary, most of them will not be able to access messages themselves.

1.3 Personal callers

Anyone expecting a personal caller should inform the receptionist who can mark it in her diary. When personal callers arrive, they should be treated with courtesy. They should be asked how they may be helped. If they have an appointment or wish to see somebody, that individual

Doc No: EM–01	ServiceCo	Date of Issue: 01.01.98
	Procedures Manual	
Approved by:		Page No 7 of 15

should be contacted straight away. If the individual is around, the receptionist should ask the caller to fill in their identity badge. The caller should then be invited to sit down while he or she is waiting. If the staff member is not available, the caller should be informed of the likely time or return and invited to wait or alternatively, to see somebody else.

Where possible, the caller should be offered tea or coffee while waiting. If there is a delay in contacting the member of staff, or if they are otherwise engaged, the caller should be kept informed.

1.4 The reception area

The reception area should be tidy at all times. The receptionist is responsible for clearing away coffee/tea cups and for tidying up magazines, newspapers and so on. A stock of the day's newspapers should be available at the seating area, together with a selection of magazines and company brochures. XXX is responsible for ensuring that the newspapers and magazines are available and up-to-date.

Callers can only enter the reception area by buzzing the intercom at the front door. If any caller leaves the reception area to go to another part of the building they should sign the register, be accompanied by a staff member and have an identity badge. It is essential for health and safety purposes that the visitor be registered as in the building.

2.0 ACCOUNTS DEPARTMENT

2.1 Sales department purchases

Parts for our sales section are bought from two sources:

- directly from the manufacturers or distributors
- as used parts from individuals and companies.

Doc No: EM–01	ServiceCo	Date of Issue: 01.01.98
	Procedures Manual	
Approved by:		Page No 8 of 15

When parts arrive into our incoming goods section, all relevant information is keyed into a computer terminal before a bar code is printed out and attached to the item or load. The barcode contains all necessary information, including item number, date, where the component is from, and so on. Each standard part type has a code number, which holds detailed information such as incoming and outgoing prices, etc.

Invoices sent in by suppliers are checked against our own database of computer processed information by the sales manager. Once everything is judged to be in order, each invoice is passed on to the financial manager for payment.

In the case of incoming used parts, the bar codes show that each item has to be assessed for pricing, depending on age, value and any work that needs to be carried out before it can be resold. These items are therefore stored separately before assessment. Once assessed, information on pricing is keyed into a computer and the barcode is updated. The payment procedure is the same as for standard items.

2.2 Sales department sales

Each member of our external sales team carries a handheld bar code reader, together with a portable computer and printer. If an item is sold and delivered immediately on a sales visit, its bar code is swiped through the reader and an invoice is printed from the computer. At the end of each day or trip, sales people download the information from their portable computers to our central networked system.

Orders are inputted on to portable computers and downloaded to the central system. Once an item leaves our central warehouse its bar code is swiped and the sales person/delivery person takes ownership of it until it is delivered.

Doc No: EM–01	ServiceCo	Date of Issue: 01.01.98
	Procedures Manual	
Approved by:		Page No 9 of 15

When payments are received they should include the relevant invoice numbers. Accounts enters the invoice number and marks it as paid. Through the database, each relevant part is then marked as paid. Our computerized sales system posts lodgement information from the manual cash book to the sales account within the debtors ledger and allocates it to the particular sale.

Within the shop, all goods are paid for on a cash basis.

2.3 Service section purchases

Service department purchases are made up of any equipment, supplies or sub-contract work needed for the carrying out the work of this section. As regards any equipment or supplies, the procedure is exactly the same as that for the sales department purchases. Sub-contractors invoice the service manager, who compares the invoice against his/her own work-sheet. Once it is approved the invoice is sent to accounts.

2.4 Service section sales

Service department sales include parts as well as repairs and servicing.

Where payment is made by cash, the money is sent to accounts. Credit sales are posted to the debtors account in the Debtors Ledger. On the last Friday of each month, debtors statements are printed out by the accounts department, and sent to the customer with a copy of the delivery docket. On the second Friday of each month a debtors listing is produced. The accounts department is then responsible for collecting outstanding accounts. After 45 days, unpaid accounts are suspended until they are paid.

Doc No: EM–01	ServiceCo	Date of Issue: 01.01.98
	Procedures Manual	
Approved by:		Page No 10 of 15

3.0 SALES DEPARTMENT

The sales department is divided into two sections:
- the external sales team of four, who deal with garages and auto shops throughout the country
- internal sales team of six, including shop staff.

3.1 Ordering of items

Purchase of new and used parts is the responsibility of the overall sales manager. All other purchases are made through the internal purchasing manager in accordance with the procedures outlined in section x.x of this manual.

A range of new and used equipment is held in stock for display, sale and demonstration. When parts need to be ordered, the person putting in the order should consult with the sales manager in preparing the specifications, agreeing an order and placing the order with the distributor. Once the order has been agreed, it is inputted to the central computer system and an order is sent out to the distributor. When items arrive in, their order number can be inputted and the incoming goods manager can check that the items tally with the order.

3.2 Receipt of incoming items

When a load or individual items arrive at incoming goods, they are inspected by the person on duty. When they are checked off against the original order, the delivery person is given a receipt printed from the computer. The person checking the items also prints off a bar code which is assigned either to the load or the individual item. This bar code includes all details such as item and order numbers, amounts, date of delivery, etc. Once the item or load is bar coded it should be placed in the

Doc No: EM–01	ServiceCo	Date of Issue: 01.01.98
	Procedures Manual	
Approved by:		Page No 11 of 15

appropriate storage area before being prepared for sale or for delivery.

In the case of used items, the delivery person will be given a receipt, but this will contain no value until the item has been assessed by the sales manager or, where appropriate, an engineer. These items are held in 'Used Pre-Assessment' until they are released into the normal warehouse.

Items or loads that are noticed to be damaged or incomplete should be appropriately marked and stored in a separate area. The invoice given to the delivery person should note the problem. At the end of each day, the sales manager should enter the computer system to find out if there have been any problem deliveries. He should then follow-up with a telephone call to the distributor. The sales manager is responsible for finding out about these problems rather than being alerted by the person in charge of checking.

3.3 Storage

New parts are stored in our warehouse or in the showroom.

3.4 Sales contract

When a sale takes place, an invoice is produced on computer. The invoice is the legal contract which includes all terms and conditions of the sale. The customer receives a copy of the invoice while the computer sends a copy electronically to the accounts department.

3.5 Final inspection and testing

In the case of certain parts and equipment, the sales assistant should carry out final inspection and testing before handing it over to the customer. See QP–32 for more details.

Doc No: EM–01	ServiceCo	Date of Issue: 01.01.98
	Procedures Manual	
Approved by:		Page No 12 of 15

3.6 Customer contact programme

The majority of ServiceCo's customers are repeat business. We currently have 72 motor garages and shops to whom we sell on an ongoing basis. We print a brochure every six months and send it out to all of our customers and to potential customers. This contains details of new stock, pricing and special offers. The sales manager is responsible for delegating the compilation and sending out of this brochure.

On a weekly basis, we look at customer contact information generated on the computer system. Customers who have not made an order in the previous three months are subsequently contacted unless they normally order less frequently.

3.7 Quality system procedures

Each manager is responsible for quality in their own departments.

The sales manager is responsible for monitoring the service provided by his/her team. He/she also represents sales staff at company quality meetings and brings up any issues regarding quality in his/her department.

He/she is responsible for ensuring that the showroom and sales offices are clean and tidy, and that all catalogue stands and specification displays are filled with up-to-date material. He/she is also responsible for ensuring that all health and safety regulations are met in his/her particular areas.

Sales staff themselves are expected to be clean and tidy, to be courteous to visitors and to give the best possible service to customers.

3.8 Control of non-conforming product

Non-conformances identified during routine inspections and audits or through complaints are dealt with by following the guidelines laid out in QP–1.

Doc No: EM–01	ServiceCo	Date of Issue: 01.01.98
	Procedures Manual	
Approved by:		Page No 13 of 15

4.0 SERVICE DEPARTMENT

The service department has a staff of seven, including the service manager who has overall responsibility for this section. Work is carried out either on ServiceCo's premises or, where necessary, on the customer's own site. We have two vans for transporting staff to customers' premises. Occasionally it is necessary to employ mechanics on a sub-contract basis – this is carried out at the discretion of the service manager.

4.1 Service contract

When a customer states his/her requirements, a job card is filled out on computer. The part is then barcoded with the relevant information and instructions. Any additional information is added as appropriate.

4.2 Control of in-house work

Any work carried out on the ServiceCo premises is supervised by the service manager, who is responsible for assigning jobs.

4.3 Control of off-site work

Any work to be carried out on a customer's premises should also be assigned by the service manager, who should give full instructions to the engineer or mechanic. Where difficulties or complications arise, details should be communicated to the service manager.

When a job is completed off-site, the mechanic should fill out an invoice in a invoice book, giving a copy to the customer if payment is received. The invoice book should be given to the service manager once the engineer arrives back at ServiceCo. Any new information should be put up on the computer by the service assistant. If payment has been

Doc No: EM–01	ServiceCo	Date of Issue: 01.01.98
	Procedures Manual	
Approved by:		Page No 14 of 15

received the invoice should be marked paid. Otherwise, the service assistant should send the customer an invoice. Any money paid off-site should be passed on to the service manager.

4.4 Service and repair standards

Any service or repair work should be carried out to the standards set out in the ServiceCo Service Manual. Staff should pay particular attention to safety. Where staff identify any additional problems to parts, they should communicate this information to the service manager or ensure that the customer is aware of the problem before any extra work is carried out.

4.5 Inspection and testing

Inspection and testing should be carried out by the service manager in accordance with QP–32.

4.6 Service manual

The service manual should reflect the range of parts being serviced and repaired by the company. It should contain the latest information from our distributors. It is the responsibility of the service manager to ensure that this is so.

4.7 Equipment

Any equipment used in the service and repairs workshop should be treated with care. It should not be taken off the premises without the permission of the service manager. While it is the service manager's responsibility to ensure that all equipment is safe and well maintained, it is each staff member's responsibility to report defects or breakages to the service manager.

Doc No: EM–01	ServiceCo	Date of Issue: 01.01.98
	Procedures Manual	
Approved by:		Page No 15 of 15

4.8 Personal protective equipment

Where required, supplied personal protective equipment should be worn.

4.9 Control of non-conforming product

Non-conformances identified during routine inspections and audits or through complaints are dealt with by following the guidelines laid out in QP–1.

Issue Identification Checklist

General

1 Do you need a licence or registration to practice part or all of your business?

2 Are you aware of the requirements on your business for
   - product/service liability
   - consumer information
   - advertising?

3 Do you have a service/customer brief fully specified or a fully specified contract(s)?

4 Do you have a code of practice or a standard for the following steps in your service procedure

- enquiry/order procedures
- supplier controls
- greeting the customer
- attending to customer
- state of store
- customer complaints and feedback?

Emissions

1   Are you in an area where there are regulations in force in relation to solid fuel?

2   Are you involved in the use of chloroflourocarbons?

3   Do you release nitrogen oxide?

4   Do you use asbestos?

Water

1   Do you release substances into water?

2   Do you discharge into sea water?

3   Do your processes involve or produce cadmium?

4   Do you discharge hexachlorocyclohexane or mercury?

Radiation

1   Do your processes involve radiation?

Nature and wildlife

1   Do your operations in any way impact on wildlife?

2   Are you involved in commercial forestry?

Nuisances and noise

1   Does your company cause noise?

2   Do you use motorized lawnmowers?

3   Does your company cause smells?

4   Does it have an unsightly premises or site?

Waste and toxic waste

1   Do your premises produce waste?

2   Do you produce polychlorinated biphenyl or polychlorinated terphenyls?

3   Is titanium dioxide used in your processes?

4   Do you use containers or liquids for human consumption?

5   Are you involved in the use or sewerage sludge in agriculture?

6   Do you use dangerous substances in batteries or accumulators?

7   Do your processes involve dangerous chemicals or substances?

8   Do your processes involve genetically modified micro organisms?

9   Do your processes involve asbestos?

10 Do you unnecessarily dump
    - paper
    - board
    - cans/containers
    - pallets
    - food
    - oils?

11   Do you produce toxic waste?

12   Do you transport, ship, store or treat waste?

Planning

1   Are you planning any extensions to your facility?

2   Have you undertaken an environmental impact assessment of any developments requiring it?

Transport, storage and distribution

1   Are you involved in the storage of dangerous substances?

2   Are you involved in the transport/transhipment of dangerous substances/hazardous waste?

Product or service

1   Do any of the following relate to your products or service
      – labelling requirements
      – packaging or waste packaging
      – product/service safety
      – legislated substances?

Health and safety

1   Are you aware of the health and safety regulations?

2   Are there procedures, training and controls in place?

3   Do you have a safety statement or a health and safety system?

Do your processes involve any of the following?	Yes/No
Veterinary products	
Cosmetic products	
Electrical equipment for use in explosive atmosphere	
Electronically hydraulically or oil electrically operated lifts	
Electromedical equipment	
Low voltage equipment	
Paints	
Semiconductive products	
Aircraft	
Toys	
Clothing and textiles	
Motor car tyres	
Footwear products	
Tableware	
Iron and steel products	
Tyre pressure gauges	
Gas	
Arsenic	
Lead	

Do your processes involve any of the following?	Yes/No
Solid fuels	
Domestic furniture	
Babies dummies/soothers	
Medical preparations	
Merchant shipping	
Hospital sterile supplies	
Pressure vessels	
Motors or motorcycles	
Construction	
Detergents	
Washing machines	
Laboratories	
Food	
Products in the EU requiring the CE Mark?	
Machinery or equipment	
Do you handle any substance covered by such legislation as dangerous substances acts?	
Do you operate in an industry with industry codes of practice – such as airline, healthcare, automobile, telecommunications, chemicals – and if so are they fully implemented?	

Index

accountability 6, 148–51
accountants
   code of practice for ISO 9000 115–16

banks
   code of practice for ISO 9000 117–18
best code of practice 74
best practice 37
BS 7750 36, 53
BSI 36, 39
BSI kitemark 46

CE Mark 31, 46, 47
CEN 36
certification 4, 37, 38
  businesses needing 74
codes of practice 4, 12, 14–15, 21,
   24–5

codes of practice for ISO 9000 85–121
codes of practice for ISO 14000 131–45
compensation 5
controls 17–18
customers
  laws relating to 12

damages 43
documentation 13-17
see also environmental management
    system documentation
see also quality management system
    documentation
see also staff health and safety
    documentation

environmental considerations 11
environmental issues 52

amenity, trees and wildlife 57
discharges to water resources 55
emissions to the air 54
energy use 58
environmental impact assessment 54
and legislation 53-4
materials use 58
noise 56
nuisances 56
odour 57
packaging/waste/litter 58
planning 54
process/public safety 57
radiation 57
urban renewal 57
waste 55–6
water supplies and sewage treatment
   55
environmental management
   documentation 125–45
   codes of practice for 131–45
   description of 125–7
   Register of Regulations 129–30
   sample environmental management
      manual 128
environmental management standard
   28
environmental management system
   51–60
   businesses needing 73
   who it affects 73
see also ISO 14000 and BS 7750
EU Machinery Directive 16
EU Misleading Advertising Regulation
   44
expert witness 5, 15, 148, 149, 150

financial mark 9
fitness for purpose 21

general dealerships
   codes of practice for ISO 9000 107
'Grand Slam recipe' 9–18

health and safety 61–7
   Department of Energy 62
   and the EU 62
   know the law 62–3
   manual 63-7
   Register of Regulations 62
   Regulations 66–7
   SOPs 65–6
hotels
   code of practice for ISO 9000 86–95

initial appraisal 21
initial environmental review 59
international management standards 5
ISO 4
ISO 9000 3-4, 15, 20, 23, 28, 30, 36,
   51–3, 60
   checklist 40–42
   and the law 30
   sectors 40
   and services 40
   and specification 38
   see also quality management
      standard
ISO 9004 Part 2 40
ISO 14000 4, 20, 23, 51–60
   definition of 59
   demand for 53
   summary 59–60
   see also environmental management
      standard
issue identification 150–51
issue identification checklist 169–74
issues 6
   see also environmental issues

law
   know the 10, 30
   customer related 30–32
   environmental 32
life cycle assessment 11

Machinery Directive 47–9
manufacturers
   code of practice for ISO 9000 99–100
misleading advertising 11, 44–5

operational issues 54
opportunism 5
outsourcing 71–2
overregulation 28

personal liability
   laws relating to 12
print and packaging
   code of practice for ISO 14000 131–4
procedures
   writing and implementing 13-17
product liability 43, 45, 52
   laws 43
product regulations 46–7, 48
product specification 10–11
public
   laws relating to 12

quality management documentation

77–121
  codes of practice for ISO 9000
    85–121
  document index 79
  list of documents 79–81
  quality manual 78–9
  sample quality manual contents 81–3
quality management standard 69–73
  not knowing you need it 72–3
  requirement by customer 69–72
  see also ISO 9000
quality management system 35–42
quality manual 40
quality procedures manual 154–68
quality service 52

Register of Regulations 27–34, 59, 63
restaurants
  code of practice for ISO 9000 118–21
retail stores
  code of practice for ISO 9000 107–12
  code of practice for ISO 14000 144–5

senior management checklist 20
service description specification 22,
  30–31
service stations
  code of practice for ISO 9000
    100–107
services
  growth in 3
  law 11
services recipe 7
shipping
  American Bureau of Shipping
    Standard 140–42

code of practice for ISO 14000
  137–43
  IMDG Code 142–3
  ISM 137–40
small business 9
solicitors/legal professions
  code of practice for ISO 9000 112–15
staff and sub-contractors 145
staff health and safety 58
  activities 16
  certain staff 16–17
  documentation 14, 15
  legislation 15
  premises and equipment 15–16
  procedures 15
  regulations 28, 29
  safety signs 17
staff training 17
statutory instruments 30, 33, 59
supermarkets
  code of practice for ISO 9000 96–9
systems
  fast track 7–18
  full system 19–25

transport industry
  code of practice for ISO 14000
    134–37

vendor management 10

waste management
  code of practice for ISO 14000 143–4
workers
  laws relating to 11

Developing Your Business Through Investors in People
Second Edition

Norrie Gilliland

- What does Investors in People involve and how would it benefit my organization?
- How can I make sure that our training and development activities will help achieve our business objectives?
- How can I encourage employees to "take ownership"?
- How do I prepare for IIP assessment?

These questions and many others are addressed in this revised edition of Norrie Gilliland's highly acclaimed book. Drawing on experience acquired working on Investors in People with more than 50 organizations, the author describes the business benefits of developing employees through systematic communication, involvement and training.

He examines the IIP national standard in detail and suggests numerous ways of meeting it, showing how to align training and development with business objectives, how to assess individual development needs and what should be the role of managers in the process. For this new edition the text has been enlarged and improved to reflect the revisions to the national standard introduced in 1997.

For managers in every kind of business, for HRD specialists and for consultants, Norrie Gilliland's book will continue to be the best available source of reference and guidance in its field.

Gower

Gower Handbook of Customer Service

Edited by Peter Murley

Foreword by Kevin Newman, Chief Executive, First Direct

In a world dominated by look-alike products at similar prices, superior customer service may be the only available route to competitive advantage. This Gower Handbook brings together no fewer than 32 professionals in the field, each one a recognized expert on his or her subject. Using examples and case studies from a variety of businesses, they examine the entire range of customer service activities, from policy formulation to telephone technique.

The material is presented in six parts:

- Customer Service in Context
- Measuring, Modelling, Planning
- Marketing Customer Service
- The Cultural Dimension
- The Human Ingredient
- Making the Most of Technology

For anyone concerned with customer satisfaction, whether in the private or the public sector, the *Handbook* is an unrivalled source of information, ideas and practical guidance.

Gower

Handbook of Customer Satisfaction Measurement

Nigel Hill

With the current emphasis on service as a competitive tool, delivering customer satisfaction has become a key strategic issue. But there's only one group of people who can tell you what the level of customer satisfaction is in your business, and that's the customers themselves. Using worked examples and real-life case studies, Nigel Hill's comprehensive guide takes you step by step through the entire process, from formulating objectives at the outset to implementing any necessary action at the end.

Among the topics covered are questionnaire design, sampling, interviewing skills, data analysis and reporting, while a set of valuable appendixes points the way to sources of further information and support. The book will equip the reader both to carry out a survey themselves and to brief and monitor an external agency for optimum results.

Whether you are directly responsible for measuring customer satisfaction or simply need to understand the issues and methods involved, the *Handbook* represents an unrivalled source of knowledge and advice.

Gower

Standards and Certification in Europe

Brian Rothery

Which standards apply to my industry? How do we obtain certification? What new standards are being developed? Where do we find out about them? With the International Standards Organization, the European Commission, and Government Agencies all developing and issuing standards and regulations constantly, it has become increasingly important to have a reliable guide.

Brian Rothery has drawn on his extensive experience of advising these bodies to write a clear explanation of the current developments in standards and certification in Europe. Particular attention is paid to describing the increasing interrelationships between the standards as the various bodies move towards creating single international standards.

The author also provides detailed information on the requirements of the various standards and related certification schemes, including practical advice on how to obtain certification and stay up to date with the standards relevant to your industry.

It is easy these days to fall foul of the increasing number of regulations, standards and advisory guidelines that govern and shape commercial activities. If you are aware of the standards, this book will show you how to keep abreast of them, and if you are not aware, you could not find a more useful guide to the increasingly regulated European business environment.

Gower